SEX, JESUS

AND THE

CONVERSATIONS

THE CHURCH

"Mo Isom is a light in the darkness with her new book, *Sex, Jesus, and the Conversations the Church Forgot*. In a world consumed and equally confused by sexuality, she refuses to remain silent, boldly addressing sex through the filter of truth found in God's Word. This book is a must-read for those tired of being pressured and deceived by culture's ever-changing view and ready to rediscover sex by its God-given meaning."

Lisa Bevere, *New York Times* bestselling author
and cofounder of Messenger International

"One of the things the church and our world need a lot more of is honesty, transparency, vulnerability, and truth all mixed together. Mo is that combination. She effortlessly blends her story with amazing truth found in Jesus. I can't recommend this book enough!"

Jefferson Bethke, *New York Times* bestselling author
and coauthor of *Love That Lasts*

"Mo is a powerful voice rising in our generation. She tells the truth, and it kills shame and invites freedom. This book will not only speak to your story but remind you of the bigger story that God is writing with our lives and our sexuality."

Annie F. Downs, bestselling author of
Looking for Lovely and *Let's All Be Brave*

"Anytime you see the words *sex* and *Jesus* on the cover of a book, you probably need to ask yourself what in the world that's about. We certainly hope that's what happens when people see this book, because the content on the inside is even more valuable than the title on the outside. Mo Isom is more than just a voice in the current cultural conversation about sexuality, God, and the church. She is a *force*. She tackles two of the stickiest subjects imaginable (sex and religion) with grace and intelligence, managing to keep the conversation reasonable and measured. She speaks with personal experience, and thus authority, on an issue that has been used as a blunt instrument to inflict damage in the current cultural wars surrounding what is right and wrong, good and bad, acceptable and unacceptable, regarding sex and faith and the church. This is an important book. We urge you to read it slowly. And you'll need a highlighter."

Clayton and Sharie King, authors of *True Love Project* and cofounders of Crossroads Camps and Crossroads Missions

"Mo writes her books as she lives her life—with authentic faith, courageous honesty, contagious joy, and a tenacious drive to make the world a better place! This book will renew your faith and reframe the way you think about sex, relationships, goals, and living life at your full potential."

Dave and Ashley Willis, bestselling authors and founders of StrongerMarriages.com

SEX, JESUS,
AND THE
CONVERSATIONS
THE CHURCH
FORGOT

SEX, JESUS, AND THE CONVERSATIONS THE CHURCH FORGOT

Mo Isom

BakerBooks

a division of Baker Publishing Group
Grand Rapids, Michigan

© 2018 by Mo Isom

Published by Baker Books
a division of Baker Publishing Group
PO Box 6287, Grand Rapids, MI 49516-6287
www.bakerbooks.com

Printed in the United States of America

Library of Congress Cataloging-in-Publication Data
Names: Isom, Mo, 1989– author.
Title: Sex, Jesus, and the conversations the church forgot / Mo Isom.
Description: Grand Rapids : Baker Publishing Group, 2018. | Includes
    bibliographical references.
Identifiers: LCCN 2017046911 | ISBN 9780801019050 (pbk.)
Subjects: LCSH: Sex—Religious aspects—Christianity.
Classification: LCC BT708 .I86 2018 | DDC 241/.664—dc23
LC record available at https://lccn.loc.gov/2017046911

Published in association with William K. Jensen Literary Agency, 119 Bampton Ct., Eugene, OR 97404

19 20 21 22 23 24   7 6

To my humble husband, Jeremiah.

Thank you for choosing me.

God's immeasurable grace comes to life in the most overwhelming ways through your love.

You stared at my past and took a knee for my future.

I am honored to be your bride.

You will always be my One and Only.

With love, your Only One

Contents

Introduction

Sex.

I don't think we're talking about it enough.

Sure, our culture is saturated with it. Our computer screens are pumped full of it. Our televisions ooze it. Our radios scream about it. Magazines and books and apps and social media outlets stream it down our throats.

Lust, body ideals, pleasure, foreplay, porn, adultery.

We're obsessed with it. We're fixated on it. We're entertained by it. We think we're deeply all-informed about it. We boast in the freedom we have to do what we want with our bodies. We tally the number of partners we've had. We're convinced it's necessary in a normal dating relationship. We're numb to the random hookups and one-night stands. We want to experience it, tease it, taste it, flaunt it, worship it . . .

But we're not willing to *really* sit down and talk about it.

While society twists, perverts, cheapens, and idolizes it, we—the church—are relatively silent about it. Awkwardly stumbling around it. Running from it. Building desperate rule lists of dos and don'ts. And, as a result, allowing the sanctity of God to be stolen by the insatiable lust of the lost.

Somewhere along the way we've allowed ourselves to be drowned out of the conversation. In a halfhearted attempt to stay relevant and relatable, we've caved in to the narrative that sex—the most prominent and overwhelming focus of our entire society—isn't for *us* to really talk about.

Right?

Wrong.

It's our responsibility to talk about it. It is our calling, as the body of believers, to share the good news of the gospel of Jesus Christ—and every version of the holy Scriptures I've ever read talks openly and candidly about sex. It is a topic fiercely close to God's heart, a topic that flows from the pages of His Word. A topic laced with affirmation, guidance, and reproof. God, after all, is the inventor of sex. We were made, by Him, as sexual beings. So if it's a topic fiercely close to His heart, it must become a topic fiercely close to ours.

I choose to speak up. Not as a preacher but as a pilgrim. A pilgrim who learned every hard lesson, every hard way. Who sinned time and time and time again in search of a pleasure I just couldn't find. Who has a mess of a testimony that was nurtured and redeemed by a King who makes our hopeless things holy.

I'll speak up for every person whose family thought their church was having certain conversations with them. The ones whose church thought their family was having certain conversations with them. The same ones who were then force-fed more than they needed to see and know by a shameless culture that couldn't have cared less about them.

I'll speak up for the teen who is tangled in the bondage of pornography. For the girlfriend feeling pressured to go further and "give it up" in order to show her boyfriend how much she loves him. For the college-aged coed who can't escape the constant temptation and stimulation on every app, website, and show. For the woman who saved herself for marriage and couldn't figure out why she felt so ashamed on her wedding night. For the wife and husband who, at times, feel like disconnected strangers between their own sheets. For the person who can so casually watch sex play out on TV and movie screens and still can't figure out why they're dissatisfied with the real thing. And for every person in between.

I'll speak up.

I'll speak up with a voice that's unashamed to stand up to a crazed and confused world and redefine sex by its God-designed meaning. A voice that's not afraid to bear my battle wounds if they help point anyone back to God's redeeming truth. A voice that's sick and tired of the world pressuring us to ride its ever-changing tide; one that's found its firm foundation in God's unchanging truth.

Reclaiming sex as the act of holy worship God always intended it to be isn't taboo or embarrassing—it's eternity-shifting. And eternity matters to me.

It's time to begin reclaiming sex for the glory of God. It's time to invite Jesus back into the bedroom. It's time to start the conversations that the church forgot. And to stand up, boldly, as a body of believers, and defend the most intimate act of worship and praise we're free to know. It's time to equip our minds and hearts with the truth of our value, our self-control, our bodies, and our relationships. It's time to start to understand and lean into the roots of why God cares so deeply about sex and be reminded that sex begins with the condition of our own hearts.

At the end of the day, in a suffocating world, the Word of God breathes boldly true. Whether you listen now, learn it the hard way later, or forever try your hardest to repress the truth, one day you will stand before the Lord and He will search your heart and know your truth. But in the meantime you have the opportunity to encounter His shame-destroying grace, have your heart perspective reframed, and find freedom in His loving reproof.

So this book is for you. I don't have all the answers. And I don't have space in these pages to address all of the different types of sexual sin struggles that are manifesting in our world and, possibly, have collided with your life too. The things I've personally experienced are all I really have any authority to speak into. I only have my testimony. But I know God uses our vulnerability for His glory, so I trust He will use these words in diverse and wonderful ways—with more intention than I could ever hope to. Please hang with me through these pages; I know there is a piece of this book for you.

If you are the weary wanderer navigating how your sexual identity and your faith become married at the cross, I hope you'll see this book through. If your perspective on sex has been shaped by the world rather than the Word for long enough, I hope my reckless and redeemed testimony will connect with you. If you're finally ready to replace perversion with purpose and pain with purity, this book, my friend, is written for you. I pray God meets you through these words, collects the pieces of your fractured story, and resurrects in your heart the beautiful reminder that He, alone, can make all things new.

1

Let's Call It Like It Is

I couldn't forget the night if I tried.

It was just one instance of one too many.

I sat on the bed while he was half-undressed and part of me wondered how on earth I even got there.

The guy I *actually* liked was in the other room, with another girl, doing who knows what.

But there I sat with his friend, who no part of me even respected, hoping that maybe if I seemed cool and low-maintenance and fun, he'd do me the favor of passing on a good word.

I rationalized away the conviction spinning through my head and once again gave in to the choice I didn't even want to make. He got what he came for. A small piece of foreplay— a halfhearted performance. I pretended to enjoy it, then lay there wondering how much longer I needed to continue to pretend I was drunk so the shame of this wouldn't feel like quite so much.

What was I doing? How did I get here? Every part of me knew that I carried more worth. I was so much more valuable than the dispensable, passed-around girl. But somehow I was back here—in the filth I'd never thought I'd find myself in. Pawning off my value in desperate hopes of feeling loved. Giving men my body in hopes they would give me their hearts.

Somehow I, the smart, well-mannered, high-achieving, "churched" girl, was drowning in my choices—a slave to sin I'd never cared to learn enough about, stuck playing the tired games of the world.

Band-Aids and Bullet Holes

I'll be the first to admit my sexual testimony is a mess.

A mess of misguidance and misbehavior, confusion and conviction, rebellion and repentance. It's a maze of boundary-pressing and power-leveraging, ignorance and impatience, lust and lost wandering. Add to the mix an overwhelming dose of overexposure, countless control issues, grief-triggered overcompensation, and a catastrophic case of insecurity. And there you have it. Me. A well-rounded girl on the surface blindly stumbling through a sin-filled battlefield within my heart.

The captain? My sin-nature. The casualty? My soul.

It's easy to see now that almost all of my sexual frustrations, bondage, and brokenness grew out of the fact that, ultimately, I knew nothing about sex.

And I mean *nothing*.

But you couldn't have told me that then. No, I lived most of my adolescence and young adulthood confidently convinced that I knew all there was to know about it. I saw what the world showed me. I listened to what the world told me. I was interested, enticed, and aware of this sex thing that seemed so delightfully imposing. I had a laundry list of thoughts, ideas, reasons, and rationalizations. On the outside I was a "good girl" from a good family, smart and well-mannered. But in my own mind I waved the proud banners of wonder and womanhood, my freedom of exploration, my right to my own body and my own sexual identity, my entitlement to dress and act as I pleased.

My moral compass often hinged on what was socially acceptable at the time, which seemed to be a more and more permissive guide as I moved through different seasons of life. In our culture, sexual expression is praised. And women, above all else, hold great power and esteem if their beauty and sexuality are enticing. After all, it's our body, our life, and our choices. That's what we are conditioned to believe and how we're conditioned to behave.

But, in truth, I knew absolutely nothing about sex.

Real sex.

That holy kind of sacrificial sex. That God-designed act of worship created to righteously unify a husband and a wife bound by the commitment of a covenant. That act that carries the weight of the cross in its wake and teaches us the power of tangling souls under a promise made before the Creator of it all. That comfort-bringing, fear-dispelling, soul-sanctifying kind of sex. That God-pleasing sex worth waiting for and celebrating, worth saving until His design designates. That all-inclusive physical, mental, emotional, and spiritual surrender.

No, I knew nothing about *that* sex.

And the church didn't talk about it either.

All the church talked about was *not* having sex, always boxing sex into the confines of dos and don'ts, rights and wrongs. Always under the awkward and tentative guise that *that* topic wasn't the most comfortable to address. They often spoke with careful, prepackaged words. Words that seemed detached from any relatability to what was *actually* going on in the world outside of those walls. It was as if they were afraid to have those types of conversations too soon—or too late. To be too honest or too mundane. As if they were overwhelmed by the tangled layers of all that topic contained and so instead kept the dialogue safe. And, I would imagine, hoped the families were diving deeper and teaching more at home.

I can hardly blame them. Not only is the topic of sex a layered, complex, and multifaceted discussion, but on top of the complexity it's already blanketed in, the world has essentially bullied the church out of the conversation. The world has so massively exalted, worshiped, and stolen ownership of all things sex-related that the church has, at times, lost footing and leverage in the fight for young people's attention. So in an effort to get even a whisper of truth into the screaming match that is the great, worldly, sexual debate, the church has often clung to the simple and clear articulation of what is sin and what is not. The rule list of what to do and what not to do.

But the infection that's grown out of that incomplete prescription is that we don't want to avoid something just because we are told to. When a list of right and wrong is all that is reinforced, we begin to see the holy and hope-filled Word of God as a rule book rather than a love letter written to our hearts. A layered and wisdom-soaked love letter gently explaining the deep-rooted *whys* that compel us to live differently from the start.

And sure, consequences are a compelling force for following the rules, but we are a generation of compartmentalized conscience. We compartmentalize our faith from our actions to serve our own desires. We often disregard the rule list and act according to impulse. Then, foolishly and soul-threateningly, we remarry the entities when they collide and get mad at God for the consequences and cause-and-effect results in our life. And we struggle with our faith—doubting the goodness of a God we never cared to actually understand or obey in the first place.

But as a result of this tug-of-war for a seat at the table in people's hearts, there is a massive conversation the church forgot, a conversation that comes from the lips of a King and begins long before the symptomatic response of promiscuity.

We've forgotten to celebrate sex as an incredible gift given to us by God and instead have solely preached against the symptoms, forgetting to address the root of it all.

As the church we've forgotten to talk about the *whys*.

We've forgotten to start from the beginning and share *why* and *what* should frame and guide our sexual understanding.

We've stood at the pulpit and shaken our frustrated fists at the world, preaching about the failings of our sexual morality and our lack of self-control, but we've forgotten to first address the aching, bleeding needs of people's hearts. We're trying to put Band-Aids on bullet holes. From bullets that never should have had the power to penetrate our God-designed souls.

We need to know the *whys* at the root of our wandering. We need to know the cause at the core of our temptation. We need to hear more than "do this, don't do that." We need to know why it matters to listen and obey in the first place. Because most of our sexual sin struggles grow out of our lack of a deep-rooted understanding of what sex is, how God sees us, why God calls us to what He does, and why obedience to that calling is worth the sacrifice. Sexual understanding, above all things, is not simply about behavior modification, it's about heart transformation. But at the beginning of heart transformation comes heart education.

So before my testimony can carry any leverage or impact, we have to get on the same page about what sex truly is, and we have to open our hearts to the *whys* that will ultimately be the only things that can compel response.

At the Root of It All . . .

It helps to start this whole sexual conversation with an accurate and perspective-shifting definition (or for many, *redefinition*) of what sex even is.

Sex is God's invention.

It's comprised of physical, mental, emotional, and above all spiritual acts of connection designed by the Creator for the unity, pleasure, and reproduction of the very lives He created. Sex is a holy gift purely designed by a God who delights in lavishing His creations with every good and perfect blessing. It is a pure act given to us as a gift to enjoy and delight in under the divine guidance of the appropriate context, circumstances, and boundaries.

Sex is an all-consuming, all-inclusive act of worship and praise. It can't stand alone as just a physical act. Or just an emotional act. Or just a mentally engaged decision. We can rationalize all day long that sex can be had in a detached manner but, in reality, we're only fooling ourselves. That argument is invalid and baseless, really, because sexual acts always tie souls. They always leave a mark—they were always intended to. Whether we carry them out within God's design is what determines whether that mark is a seal or a scar, because sexual acts were designed to bind two people. In the God-designed context between a husband and a wife, sex is one of the most powerful agents of unification, devotion, and surrender. But outside the guidelines God designated for His own invention, sexual acts become sin. And sin only ever serves to unhinge.

Physically, sex includes a beautiful range of acts and expressions. Mentally, sex is a catalyst for the activation of unbelievably powerful neurotransmitters in our minds. Emotionally, sex is an expression of love, surrender, trust, and sacrificial service to another. And spiritually, sex is a tangler of souls, a bonding agent that leaves a permanent imprint on our hearts and our spirits.

Sex is powerful. And purposeful. And as simple as it is deeply complex.

It is the most incredible and freeing gift—in the appropriate context.

But when we simplify or cheapen or commercialize sex as anything less than what it truly is and what purpose it serves in God's absolute and perfect design, we open a Pandora's box of ways that our minds, our hearts, our bodies, and our souls can be trivialized.

My research for this book was absolutely dizzying. The statistics I found reflecting young people's exposure to, perceptions of, and practices of many things that fall under the sexual umbrella were as varying and confused and extreme and daunting as you could imagine. What they summarized for me was a clear and undisputable fact that we, as a culture, have very mixed perspectives, opinions, and definitions of sex, as well as what qualifies as sexual sin. And the sources of those definitions are about as unreliable, misinterpreted, and widely varying as the numbers they reflect.

But before we get all high-and-mighty as Bible-believing Christians and think that somehow our demographic is exempt from the nauseating stats and figures, prepare for a reality check, because professed Christians are the very ones who comprise some of the most startling stats. And it all serves as evidence that even the church is missing the mark in teaching biblical literacy about sex, as a whole.

Did you know that 96 percent of young adults, professed evangelical Christians included, are either encouraging, accepting, or neutral in their view toward pornography, and don't see the use of porn as a sin? As a result, in 2016 alone, people watched 4.6 billion hours of pornography *at just one website* (the biggest porn site in the world). That's 524,000 years of porn or, if you will, around 17,000 complete lifetimes.[1]

In. One. Year.

Another study conducted in 2016 found that 82 percent of teens desire to have only one partner for life but also found that only 3 percent of Americans actually wait to have sex until marriage. Just 3 percent. (And, sadly, as you'll learn through the pages of my story, just because someone waited to have intercourse until their wedding day in no way guarantees they never struggled with other types of sexual sin.[2])

For women utilizing online dating platforms, 33 percent admit to having had sex on their very first online dating encounter.[3] And one third of the young adult population between the ages of 20–26 admit to having posted nude or seminude content online.[4]

From 2012 to 2016, 41.2 percent of women conceived pregnancies out of wedlock. And in 2014 alone, there were 1,609,619 out-of-wedlock births.[5]

There are so many more facts and figures and numbers and polls that serve to showcase the current sexual climate of our society, but what these types of stats scream to me are two primary things: First, you are not alone in your sexual wandering; 97 percent of us (and I think it's safe to say a decent chunk of that remaining 3 percent) know the power of sexual temptation, lust, desire, and action outside of God's design. So if it's any solace right from the start, you're not the outlier. You haven't gone farther or done more or seen the worst repercussions compared to anyone else. And I'm in your boat. I know I've had my share of struggles too. I hope I can weave my words together well enough throughout this book that you close the cover knowing you are understood and loved. Redemption finds us where we are, and it's waiting here for you. It sits among the 97 percent and offers hope.

Second, I'm reminded in looking at these numbers that these stats and figures and polls are just symptoms. They are evidence that, in the midst of a sex-saturated world, we do not know as much about sex as we think. Because if we deeply understood the physical, mental, emotional, and, above all, spiritual definition of and implications of sex, I don't think these numbers would look anywhere near the same. I don't think they could.

Education can't help but lead to revelation, and revelation can't help but lead to transformation when we accept God's definition as truth. Understanding God's design of sex, and the fact that it is far, far more than a physical expression, can't help but compel us to understand there is weight in the act.

There are lifelong and even eternal implications at stake. There are either life-draining or life-training practices at work in the process, depending on how we handle ourselves sexually. There is heavy significance in the heart condition we carry as we move through our days.

We are sexual beings, because sex is a deep and instructed desire in our hearts. God placed it there. But if we do not know the holy premise behind the pleasure, we become ill-equipped to handle temptation, ill-armored to fight sexual fixation, and ill-willed toward a God who we think demands obedience for the empty sake of obeying moral law.

Understanding and appreciating the true definition of sex and God's design must be followed by understanding and appreciating the *whys* that compel us to care. Because the *what* and the *whys* strengthen one another. The *what* equips our minds, but the *whys* compel our hearts. Our sexual perspectives will never be compelled to change until the *whys* catapult our heart conditions to change first.

||||||||||

God's will is for you to be holy, so stay away from all sexual sin. Then each of you will control his own body and live in holiness and honor— not in lustful passion like the pagans who do not know God and his ways. (1 Thess. 4:3–5)

2

The *Whys* Where We Must Begin

I didn't begin with the intent to sin.

I rounded one too many bases with one too many baseball players during my early years in college. I lacked any and all discretion. I desperately chased my need for shallow affirmation. And, ultimately, I made myself available to anyone who wanted a piece of me. The baseball team seemed to be my niche, and before I knew it I had built a reputation that preceded me.

It's humiliating to look back and realize I was the girl being passed around. I thought for sure, at the time, that I was in the driver's seat. I wanted, so deeply, for one of them to choose me. To *really* choose me. I didn't enjoy the casual nature of it all. I deeply wanted a relationship and genuine connectivity. But all I knew was how to use my sexuality as a tool—my first line of seduction in hopes I could eventually snag one of their hearts too.

I was a wounded woman. I had struggled with my identity for years, recently and unexpectedly lost my father to suicide, and was in a season of running as far and as fast as I could from God. That's not to wrap any excuses around my behavior but rather to illustrate just a few of the countless factors that layered themselves underneath the shell of a girl who was always a good time at the bar. Desperate girls do desperate things when they don't feel loved. And no matter how hard I tried to craft my image on the surface, sexual sin was the enticement I always let in.

Those early years in college were the darkest and most shame-filled years of my life, sexually. They were the height of my sexual deviance, my dark internal struggles, and my imprisonment to sin. But do you notice how *that* climax is only given rights to sit at the start of my story? The shame and embarrassment and reputation and repercussions of those dark nights under different sheets don't get any authority over me or the pages of my story. Because their peak in my life ultimately looks like a ripple in a pond compared to the colossal tsunami of Christ's glory that pulled me out of my brokenness.

I've spent a lot of time thinking back to why I made so many of the choices I did throughout my life—plenty of poor and misguided decisions that you'll read about in these pages. But the more I've thought back on my sexual journey, the more I realize that beneath layers and layers of symptomatic, sinful behavior rested the fundamental truths I completely missed, or others missed in teaching me, as I grew.

In truth, my sexual struggles began long before any type of sexual activity. My promiscuity and deep soul wounds grew out of a heart that was out of tune. My tossed-around, inhibitions-down, performance-based cry for love never began with a conscious decision that sexual acts were something I wanted or needed, regardless of truth. No, I began by missing the simplest, most basic fundamentals about the very person staring back at me in the mirror. I wonder if that's where your sexual sin began too.

God's First Command and Our Inherent Worth

God's Word is full of stories, lessons, teachings, parallels, and anecdotes about sex. It's kind of amazing. I don't think I ever realized how much sexual content was in the Bible until I began to marry faith and sexuality in my heart and seek out what God actually had to say about it all. That wasn't until the end of my time in college, and I wish, constantly, I had paid attention sooner. Because tuning in to what God has to say about all that falls under the umbrella of sex is like discovering the blueprint for a layer of ourselves and our human nature we didn't even know existed. It is a revelatory piece of the *why* that can compel us to live differently, and it sat on my bookshelf and bedside table collecting dust while I wandered aimlessly through misguided sexual struggles and lust.

In fact, the beginning of a deeper understanding of the beauty and significance of sex is found in the first few pages of Scripture. Some of God's very first words over human-kind were about our inherent value as His creations, and about this act He created called sex. God, Himself, wasted no time. I think that's why I find it funny when I hear that some think, as Christians, we're too pure to talk about these types of things. Conversations about sex mirror the first holy conversation God ever held with humans. To talk about sex openly as a body of believers is to look more and more like the King who created it.

Genesis 1:27–28 simply says, "So God created human beings in his own image. In the image of God he created them; male and female he created them. Then God blessed them and said, 'Be fruitful and multiply. Fill the earth and govern it. Reign over the fish in the sea, the birds in the sky, and all the animals that scurry along the ground.'"

When I read this Scripture, my heart dives in so much deeper than the few words on the page. I see the beginnings of a love letter written to our hearts about who we are, whose we are, and what God has for us.

So God—the Creator of the heavens and the earth . . . the One who placed the stars in the sky and formed each and every beautiful, complex creature . . . the One who set the waves in the sea and rolled the land with hills and valleys . . . the One who painted day in the sky and appropriated night . . . the One who formed this massive, sprawling, incomprehensible world and every tiny detail within it . . . formed **you.** *Above all other creations, He created* **you.** *As the pinnacle of His work. No other creature was formed in His image. No other creature given authority to rule over and care for the rest of His construction. But* **you.** **Us.** *Both man and woman. Made equally in His form, with neither man nor woman being made more in the image of God than the other. But both being made in His perfect and unique design. And when He looked at what He made, He was SO well pleased. When He looks at* **you,** *He stands in awe of His work. He blessed us, and in as gentle a tone as a Father and as powerful a tone as the unparalleled Creator, He first spoke, "Be fruitful and multiply. Fill the earth . . ."*

"Be fruitful and multiply . . ." Be productive, constructive, and useful. Be beneficial, be gainful, be effective. Don't get distracted.

Be all that I formed you to be in My image. Trust My design. Know that I know far more detail about your heart and your body than you can even conceive. And as you live a life in worship and wonder of My beautiful work, multiply. Delight in this pleasure I pour out to you. Come together as I have designed you, follow the instruction that I will give you, and in an abiding, blessed, and covenantal love . . . multiply for the glory of God.

This is not to put words in God's mouth but to put context in your heart. You, your body, and your life were created with purpose. If we are creatures made in His image, above all other creatures on earth, then our bodies are sacred in His sight. And if God wasted no time in addressing sex, then there must be holy context to the act. A holy context that marries our inherent value with our God-instructed sexual rights.

✳ Our immeasurable worth as image-bearing creations of God and our sexual identity have been unified since the beginning of creation. And if we learn about one but not the other, or value one above the other, we unwind two truths about our very nature that were never meant to know divide. When we compartmentalize and unhinge the two, we rob ourselves of the unifying identity assigned to both from the beginning. And as a result we stumble into sexual sin struggles because we're searching for the very thing we dislocated from sexual obedience at the start—our value. <u>We use sexual power and prowess and pleasure to search for affirmation and love because we've unknowingly cut ourselves off from the true affirmation and love we have already received from the start.</u> We fail to see our own worth so we search for someone to assign it to us. We seek attention and praise—missing all that God has already said about us. Longing to know and feel that we're worth something because we never knew we were originally worth everything through God's incredible design.

The *why* simply begins there.

With you. And me.

Why does it matter what we do with our bodies and who we connect our lives with, sexually? Because you and I were created by a King, a King with specific guidance and direction for us. A King who is incapable of creating worthless things. We were created in the image of God. In that perfect image, created with everything *of* God—everything wonderful and spiritual and eternal—stamped into our DNA.

We are not just *here*, we are *His*.

And that changes everything.

Psalm 139:13–14 sings, "For you created my inmost being; you knit me together in my mother's womb. I praise you because I am fearfully and wonderfully made; your works are wonderful, I know that full well" (NIV).

If you are one of His works, what does that say about you? We were created with immeasurable worth, value, beauty, and purpose. We were fearfully and wonderfully made. We were placed on this earth for such a time as this and we are worth more than I think we realize. We don't need a partner to assign us a value when we feel worthless. We need a soul reawakened to its worth in the Father's eyes. Our value is found in the very image in which we're made. We are God's greatest design. And it's due time we started clinging to this truth and disciplining this belief into our minds.

Our actions are significant and carry more purpose than we recognize. And there is more significance to our sexual expression than we realize. All that falls under the umbrella of sex has meaning and purpose in God's design. The way you carry yourself and who you give yourself to is ultimately a reflection of the value you assign to His creation in you.

We are worth more than the world's confused games, more than the world's trial-and-error sexual maze. We must believe that if God's very first instruction to humanity involved identity, sex, and a commissioning of purpose, then there is far more to sex than the guessing game the world invites us to publicly play. The world invites us to put our bodies, our emotions, and our naivety on display as we navigate the web it has woven to satisfy the insatiable lust of the lost. But the Word invites us to so much more.

If we aren't aware of our deep-seated value and worth in God's eyes at our creation, then the temptation to define our own identity will always rob us of the purity called from us first.

Choosing to Choose for Ourselves

Another layer of understanding the *why* is understanding the role we play in why sexual misunderstanding, temptation, and deviance run so rampant in our hearts. If sex was a gift given to us by God, pure in its intent and edifying of our worth, then why is it also the source of so much dissension, obsession, abuse, and hurt? When did sex go from virtue to vice? The answer lies within the very same creation God so fearfully and wonderfully designed.

We were creatures made to worship.

God, Himself, created us with the desire to worship coursing through our hearts. It is a predisposition—inherent and ingrained and eternal. And there was and is nothing flawed in God's design.

Our struggles, then, don't originate from our ingrained desire to worship; they originate from *what* we choose to worship in our lives, because it's no mystery that we are all worshiping something. Someone. Some dream. We were made to exalt, but somewhere along the line we became willing to exalt *anything*.

It's important we first understand where our broken exaltation began, because humankind never intended to be *bad*. We, as a culture—and often as a church—have somehow bought into the hard-and-fast belief that sin is as simple as bad versus good, wrong versus right, hate versus love. When, in actuality, sin is far more complex than that. Sin never entered into the world because people intentionally chose to be bad.

As God's perfect and crafted creations, given the freedom of choice from a loving Creator, we didn't revolt with the desire to be *bad* people; we revolted with the desire to be our *own* people. And all that could come from that was the bad and the broken we wrestle with now. We revolted as His people to become our own people, and through the course of history we've rarely looked back since.

The original sin in the Garden of Eden didn't look like Eve consciously deciding she was going to be bad and sin rather than obey the instruction of God. The original sin looked like Eve curiously choosing for herself, despite God's instructions. In our lives, our sin doesn't usually look like an intentional decision to be bad; it almost always looks like a subconscious choice to choose for ourselves what is best for us, what we desire, and what we think we want and need.

We are creatures made to worship. But because we are fallen, because we rebelled, we quickly choose to worship ourselves, and that is where our sexual sin begins—not in choosing to be bad but choosing to be our own, despite recognizing we were created as His.

Regardless of social class, race, or culture, sex uniformly seems to become one of the first things we choose to choose for ourselves. Though sex was created as an act of worship toward God, we waste no time in making it its own god and worshiping at the throne of our wants. From pornography to masturbation to promiscuity to lust. We've chosen to choose for ourselves. And, if we're being honest, without being armored up with the wisdom or experience to recognize the repercussions of these things, these are all things we *want*.

Don't get me wrong; our society will work its hardest to convince us there's nothing wrong with this. We have a living, breathing Word of God spelling out exactly what is best for us—exactly what will guard our hearts, what we can place our faith in and rely on, what will lead us in the way we should go. But we have a culture coaxing us to close that book, to muffle that Truth, and to instead worship our own bodies and minds whenever, however, and with whomever we choose.

We have the *Word* telling us: Be careful! "The human heart is the most deceitful of all things, and desperately wicked. Who really knows how bad it is?" (Jer. 17:9).

While we have the *world* telling us: No, no, the heart wants what it wants. Follow your heart, trust your feelings, put all your stock in your own emotions.

We have the *Word* telling us: "The temptations in your life are no different from what others experience. And God is faithful. He will not allow the temptation to be more than you can stand. When you are tempted, he will show you a way out so that you can endure" (1 Cor. 10:13).

While we have the *world* telling us: The temptation and the tease are a part of the pleasure. You can't help what you're attracted to and you can't help giving in to your physical desires. It's sexual attraction. Clearly your body wants it, so why not have it? It's your life.

We have the *Word* telling us what will lead us in the way we should go: "God's will is for you to be holy, so stay away from all sexual sin. Then each of you will control his own body and live in holiness and honor—not in lustful passion like the pagans who do not know God and his ways" (1 Thess. 4:3–5).

While we have the *world* telling us: Sexual immorality is subjective to opinion. You're going to abstain? Are you going to wait until you're married and never try anything sexually first? Good luck keeping a boyfriend or girlfriend if you're not going to be physical with them along the way.

For every unchanging Word of Truth, we have an opinion of the world. For every call to obey and worship God first, we have a temptation to not forget about ourselves. For every secure and loving command from God, we have an insecure world, frantic and failing, proclaiming, "No! Choose for yourself! You are your own. You are in control."

So we sit in our sin and we desperately worship the wreckage— trying to force it to feel like *enough*. God's own people, who somewhere along the line choose, instead, to become our own people, the world's people. And just like that the sexual desires placed within us become the sexual fixations of our rebellious hearts.

Because we choose to choose for ourselves.

Our design and our rebellion. They are two of the strongest roots at the core of our *why*. When we open our hearts and minds to understand the unwavering value God knit into us, as women and as men, and the sin-nature that consumes us in our fallen, broken state, we can start to see the source of our tensions and frustrations. When we miss the design we can rationalize the rebellion. When we miss the wonder of our worth we sell short the weight of our wandering. Our *why* must begin with our equal understanding of these two colliding forces in our lives. And when the time comes for us to either armor up and fight for our purity or give way to the rushing, temptation-filled tide, we must decide whom we will serve. Time after time after time.

So what are we worshiping? Sex is a beautiful and powerful gift, in the proper context of its intent. But I wonder, today, how many of us have never known it was meant to be that way? I wonder how many of us have chosen to choose for ourselves, and have recklessly given pieces of ourselves away?

I know that was my story. Never with the intent to be bad. Never with the intent to rebel. But simply with the intent to keep up with the world and what it coaxed out of me. With the intent to explore my body and allow it to be explored by others in hopes of someone praising my beauty. With the intent to pacify the urges of pleasure and lust and desire inside of me.

Not overtly, at first. Not to any great extreme. But my lack of understanding about my inherent worth and my insatiable curiosity called me to choose for myself, and that welcomed me down a path of sin-filled sexual wandering.

||||.||||

They traded the truth about God for a lie. So they worshiped and served the things God created instead of the Creator himself, who is worthy of eternal praise! (Rom. 1:25)

I AM A CREATED THING.

35

3

Virginity, Purity, and the Gray Area In Between

I can clearly remember the day.

I was sitting on the edge of a red loveseat in my parents' bedroom. It's where my mom and I had most of our best talks. Where the sun beamed in and scorched the color off the fabric on the back of that little two-person couch. I grew up in a conservative, well-monitored, Christian home, with two loving parents and a sharp older sister. We were the classic, middle-class, nuclear family with access to great education and a comfortable church. Our house tucked itself right inside a semicircle of neighbors' homes. There were kids and teens who lived all around us—some a great influence, and some not so much.

At that point in my life, I had already been exposed to pornography, and sex was very much already on my mind. In the late '90s there were fuzzy channels you could find on TV where porn was just distinguishable if you squinted your eyes and tilted your head far enough. I had stumbled across friends' parents' *Playboys* at their homes and already had an older neighbor tell me everything she knew about sex and foreplay and masturbation and boys. On top of it all, I had also started to figure out that certain things felt good on my body.

I was only nine years old.

I don't think my sweet mom knew all that I had been exposed to, but she wasn't naive either. She was the world's best mom for honest conversations and overexplanations and subtle interrogations to keep tabs on me. She was also always very open about sex. She wasn't hesitant to talk to me about things other parents shied away from or danced around with their young preteens. But that day when my questions shifted from logistics on how snakes could possibly have sex (I was working on a science presentation that just wasn't adding up, and to be honest I'm still confused on that one) and instead started to creep toward one too many overly illicit topics, I remember her sitting me down and looking at me with an endearing anxiousness. (I'm sure if I had a nine-year-old tossing around terms like I probably used, I would be a bit panicked too.) But she found the simplest words she could at the time and explained to me that sex was meant to be shared between a husband and a wife. That God desired for us to be virgins when we marry, meaning we have not had sex with anyone else. She shared with me that both she and my dad were virgins when they married and had only had sex with each other. And that when you have sex, you can become pregnant. And that is how my sister and I were born and how families are formed.

For a girl who idolized her parents and yearned to make them proud, I had heard all I needed to hear. I don't think a moment passed before I stood up from the couch and boldly stated, "Then, Mommy, I promise to be a virgin until I'm married too!" And with a quick twist and a tightened upper lip, my nine-year-old mind made up, I triumphantly marched out of the room.

I didn't give her time to explain much else. And I suppose to a mom trying to keep things simple for a little girl, that day was a small victory.

But at the time, my youth, my haste, and my mom's unintentionally oversimplified explanation became the first few ingredients in a muddied mixture of incomplete understanding about sex as a whole.

The Vain Virginity Vow

The biggest issue was that my search for deeper sexual understanding ended abruptly with my vow of virginity. My mind shelved the need for any more information about sex when I began to believe that I knew all I needed to know. My decision was made. And at such a young age there was nothing tempting me to break that vow.

There was also a sense of pride that came with the title of *virgin*. I wore it like a badge of honor. It was something I could control—a distinctive factor that set me apart—and a title I gradually owned and even flaunted, as if it somehow amplified my righteousness for people to praise. The church exalted it, as well. So, to me, being in line with my parents' wishes and in line with the church's instruction made me feel like that much better of a person—like that much "better" of a Christian.   *pride*

I rolled my eyes in my own smugness at a culture and media that portrayed virginity as such a taboo thing. I never "got" why girls were trying to lose their virginities by prom, or handing over their bodies to their first boyfriend to prove to him they loved him enough. I wasn't ever on board with the hype behind guys racking up their "number," and the double standard of girls being labeled if they gave themselves away just as freely. Honestly, it just all seemed messy. And if I'm being transparent here, it all felt *beneath me.* So I proudly waved my flag of abstinence and arrogantly exalted my intact virginity.

I didn't realize this at the time, but my obedience to God's design and instruction in my sexual decisions wasn't carried out as an act of reverence and humility; it was carried out as a demonstration of my self-righteous abilities. And that sustained me for a while, but my vow of virginity started to become my own self-constructed stumbling block when suddenly the sexual temptation I had pridefully scoffed at others for wrestling with began to tempt me.

It started innocently enough. I was alone. I was human and felt normal, natural urges. And it was *my* body. As far as I knew, masturbation had no effect on my virginity. So I could still wade into the water there and not be violating my vow.

Soon enough, that sexual exploration evolved into nervous first kisses and make-out sessions if the newest boy I was interested in at the time and I could sneak away and find a private place. No effect on my virginity.

Then one day their hands found the courage to wander and new feelings overcame me, and even though there were nerves within me that knew I was doing more than I should, I rationalized that it still had no impact on my virginity.

And then the hands got more aggressive, and more and more was expected of me. And I never once felt like I knew what I was doing, but why would I give less of myself since I had already been this far with other boys? I felt like performance was expected of me. And, after all, I was still a virgin. I still had my virginity.

Eventually, when oral sex came into the equation, I was already in the throes of promiscuity and stopped keeping track of my comfort level or my apprehensions or my dignity. I wrestled with tension and conviction, knowing it was all too much and too far, but my convicted pride rationalized that I still technically had my virginity. Right?

I pushed the envelope time and time and time again. In recent years, I've had so many Christian girls ask me if anal sex still qualifies them as a virgin. I'm never shocked or taken aback by that question because, to be honest, it was one my own mind toyed with often in that time too.

I eventually got to the point of bargaining, "How far is too far?" "How far can I go to still qualify as a virgin?" "What even counts as *real* sex?" My efforts to rationalize were almost impressive, looking back. Soul-stealing and life-compromising, but dogged. Isn't it amazing how adaptable our hearts are to harboring sin? Our sin-nature is like a chameleon, disguising itself to look however it needs to look in order to make us feel like our sin isn't *too* much. *Too* far. *Too* messy. As if sin has a grading scale we can negotiate. We always could be worse, couldn't we?

"How far is too far?" was my constant question. And for my answer I didn't look to the Word, I looked to the world. Because the world's response fed my raw wants first.

So I spent years giving pieces of myself away, sexually, all while flying my virgin banner high and halfheartedly rationalizing that I still held my virginity. And I would lie in my own emotional filth in a college bed filled with lust and regret, and

I would wonder why they would whisper and laugh to themselves when I told them we couldn't go *all* the way because I was a virgin. Yet, like a fool, I would roll over and give pieces of myself away to make sure my newest friend knew I could still meet all of his other needs. And to help stomach the lump of conviction I felt in my throat, I would tell myself that it was my body, my right, and my freedom to choose what I wanted to do. I told myself I was powerful, I was in control, and I was even well disciplined for not giving him everything.

Looking back, I was living out the flawed logic Paul warned us against in 1 Corinthians 6:12 and I didn't even realize it.

> You say, "I am allowed to do anything"—but not everything is good for you. And even though "I am allowed to do anything," I must not become a slave to anything.

I was trying to preserve my "virginity" while still doing what I wanted to do. I was trying to have my cake and eat it too. Before I even knew what had hit me, I was empty. And broken. And owned by temptation and lust. Sure, I had the freedom and right to do everything I was choosing to do, but it wasn't all beneficial for me. I ended up a slave in chains trying to convince myself I was free. But my sexual appetite could no longer be satisfied by anything less than as far as I'd already gone by that point. And I despised myself for it at times. But I stood up each new morning with a righteous chip on my shoulder—because I may have had a list, and a past, and plenty to be ashamed of—but on my wedding day I could still say I was a "virgin."

Surely that was *enough*. Right?

The idea of virginity. It messed with me. And why should we ever expect that it won't?

Because solely holding on to the thing that is virginity can become a vow made in vain. A works-based answer to a life-surrender question. God doesn't want your self-reliant promise of virginity. He wants your whole heart, with abstinence being a willing by-product of your love for His instruction and your faithfulness to abide. But in our self-serving sin we respond, "How about instead of my whole heart I just give you some semi-good behavior?" Then we desperately cling to the hope that, no matter how muddy our hearts, that credential looks clean on the surface. And counts for something.

You know we're only fooling ourselves, right?

The narrow focus of virginity is just the surface layer, under which God is inviting us to immeasurable depths of wisdom, freedom, and love. A one-dimensional focus on virginity robs us of the depth of our own soul's yearning for intimacy and its deep desire for abiding worship and worth. No, God doesn't solely call us to virginity. God calls us, in all ways, to purity and the power of its incredible purpose in our lives.

The Purpose of Purity

Purity.

There's another layer of the *why* we've missed along the way.

And one I genuinely can't remember anyone talking to me about in a relatable way.

Purity.

The deeper, wider, broader heart condition that God actually cares about. Purity that stretches beyond our sexual choices and encompasses every facet of our lives. Purity that naturally compels abstinence as a beautiful by-product but is wider reaching than just our physical sexual activity.

For years of my life, and woven all through my story, I proudly proclaimed the shallow vow of virginity but completely missed the greater, God-honoring concept of purity. I made my prepubescent promise and even wore a ring. I was praised by other Christians for my proud and loud virginity. But all the while I was ultimately missing the point. I was flaunting the title and halfheartedly living out the call to action based on my own willpower and strength, without actually knowing why I was denying myself and why it mattered that I turn away from certain things. And because of that, every time temptation came, my willpower grew weaker and my wants grew stronger. Until eventually my tankful of self-motivation ran on empty and temptation, lust, and pressure owned me. My sexual decision-making was built on the manmade sands of righteousness and rule-following rather than being rooted in the God-designed rock foundation of a pure heart seeking to honor a King who loved me.

But how could it have been? I had missed the *why.*

I had been preached to about virginity, coached in the dos and don'ts. But a conversation about the bigger picture of purity compelling those choices? That was one the church forgot.

And, admittedly, one I hadn't sought.

I think my parents assumed the church was pointing me toward the bigger concept of purity, and the church assumed my parents were covering that ground. But the fact of the matter is that it wasn't a conversation I broached with my family because I didn't know it was one I should have. And the church stayed so tight-lipped, so nervous as to what age they were supposed to begin to navigate such a taboo concept that once they did start talking about sex and abstinence it was simply through the fearful approach of "You have to wait," which wasn't all wrong. But harping on avoidance seemingly for its own sake did little to prepare me for when rule-following seemed mundane and what I was doing still felt permissible when I asked myself, "Do I still count as a virgin if I don't go *all* the way?" When we exalt virginity as the goal and disassociate how purity plays any role, it's way too easy to lose ourselves in that gray area in between.

I had missed the three most beautiful layers of purity. I had missed (1) the purity in God's design and design of me, (2) the purity in His redemption of me through Jesus, and (3) the true purpose of His call to purity in my conduct as a vessel He desired to use.

First Corinthians 6:13–20 summarizes the big picture of purity so clearly:

> You say, "Food was made for the stomach, and the stomach for food." . . . But you can't say that our bodies were made for sexual immorality. They were made for the Lord, and the Lord cares about our bodies. And God will raise us from the dead by his power, just as he raised our Lord from the dead.
>
> Don't you realize that your bodies are actually parts of Christ? Should a man take his body, which is part of Christ, and join it to a prostitute? Never! And don't you realize that if a man joins himself to a prostitute, he becomes one body with her? For the Scriptures say, "The two are united into one." But the person who is joined to the Lord is one spirit with him.
>
> Run from sexual sin! No other sin so clearly affects the body as this one does. For sexual immorality is a sin against your own body. Don't you realize that your body is the temple of the Holy Spirit, who lives in you and was given to you by God? You do not belong to yourself, for God bought you with a high price. So you must honor God with your body.

The first layer of purity originates from a pure and holy God. A God who is perfect in every way. Purity is first displayed in God's beautiful creation of us, people made in His image. Our bodies are fearfully and wonderfully formed by the Maker of the heavens and earth as works of art—vessels for His worship and work. And inside these incredible carrying agents we were given as bodies are souls God loves even more. Souls created to be united with His perfect purity in all ways, all things, and all phases of our life on earth and our eternal life in heaven.

Because of God's perfect and unobstructed purity, impurity and immorality simply can't exist in His presence. He is too holy. Too faultless. Too righteous to coexist with darkness. So impurity in our lives separates us from a perfectly pure God.

But God loves us so much and desires reconciliation with us. He loves us so deeply that even in our rebellion, He made a holy and perfect sacrifice on our behalf; a way for our sins to be paid for and hope to be restored in our lives. Our lives were resuscitated at the cross when God's purity collided with the very sin that first tore us apart. Our sin separated us from Him. But our ransom was paid. Through the perfect life, death, and resurrection of Christ, our lives and our bodies were bought back from the grip of death at a holy price. And as a result of the Father's love for the heart of humanity—as broken and messy and confused as we are—our purity should also be compelled out of our gratefulness for His immeasurable grace.

The third and most incredible and humbling part of the deeper call to purity is that God then goes so far as to use us—the once-rebellious wanderers—as the carriers of His Holy Spirit, His love, and His light.

When we accept the sacrifice Jesus made for us, our bodies become vessels for the Spirit of the very God who is perfectly pure and full of light. We become physical temples for His presence, His power, and His offer to all of eternal life.

We are called to purity because we are the very vessels responsible for reflecting God's truth, His love, and His instruction and design to the world. When we place our faith in that King who hung on that cross, and when we ask Him to fill our hearts, to be our strength and our guide, we voluntarily empty ourselves of ourselves and open up our bodies, our words, and our hearts to carry His light.

God cares deeply about the obedience and purity of the hearts that carry that light. He cares about the heart of each person long before He cares about their actions. Because our actions are what grow out of a pure or impure heart. When our hearts are pure, our actions become pure. And when our hearts are impure, our actions follow suit. God desires that we be pure in heart so our actions don't result in sin when we are the very vessels He has entrusted His Spirit with.

> God's will is for you to be holy, so stay away from all sexual sin. Then each of you will control his own body and live in holiness and honor—not in lustful passion like the pagans who do not know God and his ways. . . . God has called us to live holy lives, not impure lives. Therefore, anyone who refuses to live by these rules is not disobeying human teaching but is rejecting God, who gives his Holy Spirit to you. (1 Thess. 4:3–5, 7–8)

He asks us to focus on purity, in all ways, so we can appropriately shine, reflect, and share that light. So when those who are lost and wandering and hurting see us and seek to see Jesus through us, they aren't confused by hypocrisy, or fake-it-till-you-make-it role-playing, or artificial "good works" we are trying to use to mask our insufficiencies. No, God desires a pure heart because that is the least clogged avenue for Him to reflect His goodness to others through and the least obstructed way for Him to pour His love, grace, and hope into us too.

What happens as a result of understanding why we are called to purity? Virginity and abstinence become the by-products of a heart that seeks to honor God. It's about so much more than doing what's right and avoiding what's wrong. It's a reflection of preserving our bodies and our hearts for a God who gave His life for us first. "God blesses those whose hearts are pure, for they will see God" (Matt. 5:8).

A pure heart compels us to make decisions that don't seek first to please ourselves but rather to please a holy God. A pure heart compels us to surrender our lives and follow His leading, even when it's hard. A pure heart compels us to take our thoughts captive, recognize our temptations, and surrender our minds and our bodies to things that are pleasing to God. A pure heart compels us to turn away from a sin-filled world and set our focus on things that bring hope and life. Actions that are uplifting and edifying and good. Choices that don't lead us wandering into gray areas but keep us on a straight and narrow course toward His glory.

God's instruction to save ourselves, sexually, for our spouse is not simply about a forced list of dos and don'ts. And it's certainly not intended to make us proud and self-righteous in our ability to obey—or not. God calls for purity from us and blesses those who are pure in heart because He loves us. And He knows—in this fallen, broken, twisted world—what is best for us. He is protecting us. He is teaching us self-control and growing endurance and vitality in us. Purity is the true *why* intended at the root of virginity. It is the greater source God always intended to be the compelling force for our actions and our discretion in all things.

And purity is something I missed, massively.

I never slowed down enough to lean into God's incredible love for me as a decision-making guide for my sexuality. His love, care, and protection of my body—that is a compelling force. His love can actually be a sustainable motivation for pure conduct, even in challenging and testing times. I set myself up for failure when I stopped seeking further knowledge or deeper sexual insight and instead, unknowingly, claimed self-righteousness and badge-earning as my source of motivation for virginity. I had missed *why* God asked me to deny myself of sexual things outside of His instruction. And as a result of my ignorance, I lost myself in the gray area in between.

I share all of this to give a look inside my own personal failings rather than to instruct or to preach. Because at nineteen years old, and with a list of shame a mile long and a vain title of virgin striving to cover it all, I met a King who said I was redeemed. And through Christ, God began to teach me that He never solely desired my virginity. He desired, above all else, my purity in all things. In my thought life, my words, my actions, and my choices. And I can't help but wonder, how many of us out there are proudly flying the flag of virginity, assuming that alone is what grows our righteousness and esteem? Or how many are just like me, touting virginity by title but compromising every step in between? I wonder, how many recognize their purity was lost long before their virginity and feel like they could never be redeemed? Or how many, for the first time, are even recognizing that there's a difference between what they thought was "good enough" and how God actually desires us to be?

Physical virginity can't be restored.

But spiritual, mental, physical, and emotional purity can.

I was overwhelmed with a life-changing, heart-transforming gratefulness the day I learned that I was forgiven for my sexual sin and that, through Jesus, my purity was redeemed.

That redemption of purity is available for everyone, even those who feel like they have lived their whole lives in the gray area in between. "And everyone who has this hope fixed on Him purifies himself, just as He is pure" (1 John 3:3 NASB).

It's time we place virginity in its rightful seat. It is a beautiful and valuable thing, but we must understand, above all else, that God yearns for a far wider-reaching purpose through our hearts and our bodies—that we would surrender fully to purity and steer clear of the gray areas in order to guard our hearts. That we wouldn't obey for obedience's sake but rather as a response to His immeasurable grace. That we would truly understand God is willing and capable of resurrecting our sexual mess for His glory. And that our questions would shift from "How far is too far?" to "Oh God, how close can I draw to You? Please draw near to me."

||||;!|||

It's not what goes into your body that defiles you; you are defiled by what comes from your heart. (Mark 7:15)

Create in me a clean heart, O God.
Renew a loyal spirit within me. (Ps. 51:10)

4

You Are What You See

I could draw you the scene.

It's still so fresh in my memory.

I lugged open the heavy door of that silver truck and a playing card fell out from the wad of papers and business cards and folders wedged behind the passenger seat. When I bent down to pick it up, my innocent eyes were filled with their first and most memorable dose of graphic pornography. I turned that card over to shove it back in the recesses of the cluttered cab and saw on it a man and a woman doing things I instantly felt dirty for even seeing. My heart wanted to pound out of my chest and my hands started to sweat as I tried my hardest to act like I hadn't seen a thing when the daddy I loved climbed into the driver's seat.

Porn—on a novelty poker card, of all things. And I, an eight-year-old little girl, was instantly consumed by shame and guilt and curiosity in what I'd just seen.

There was more stashed in the back of my dad's truck, and as much as I was shocked and confused and hurt that he would be looking at anyone else naked besides my mommy, I couldn't get the images out of my head. Before long my curiosity and confusion led me to search for whatever else I could find when nobody was looking. Cards in his truck, magazines in his office—it wasn't hard to find more of the filth and the porn and the nudity. In fact, the more I began to pay attention, the more I realized <u>this was a prominent thing in my dad's life.</u> There were times I'd come downstairs in the middle of the night for a glass of water and turn the corner to see my dad watching graphic things on the TV that kept him out of the arms of my mommy. One too many times I'd stride into our home office and see him quickly and anxiously turn off the computer screen. And then there was an instance I'll never forget when he accidentally programmed the timing wrong on our TV, and a prompt for the pornographic movie he had purchased suddenly popped up in the middle of the afternoon cartoon I was watching.

Suddenly porn was at the forefront of my mind and I felt, to a degree, like it was almost calling out to me. I hated that I was so interested. I felt guilty for the curiosity that lingered in me. But I was already growing an appetite for the interest and stimulation I felt when I stumbled across those things I wasn't supposed to see. And the sin struggle of another wasted no time in captivating the interest and attention of a previously oblivious preteen.

That's where trying to watch it on the fuzzy cable channels began. That's where reckless searches on the internet and nervous scrolling through perverse sites started for me. Before I was even a teenager, all of the things that bound and plagued the mind and heart of my daddy were steadily coercing my mind and heart too.

My occasional nervous internet clicks evolved into more bold, obsessive searching. The amount of time I spent thinking about sexual things increased. I started drawing nude images, trying to imitate the things I saw, and experimenting with masturbation. As a not-even-preteen.

I idolized the seeming allure and the power of the women on the screens. They seemed so in touch with their sexuality, so in control of their bodies, so bold and brazen in expressing their pleasure and their ability to give the men whatever they wanted or needed. The conviction I felt while I watched things was heavy, but I told myself in the moment that I was a virgin. I wasn't doing anything wrong because I wasn't actually doing any of those things with anyone else. I convinced myself there was nothing wrong with watching these women in order to "learn a few things." In fact, I told myself, studying what these women did—what love and sex must really look like and be like—would be beneficial for me. Then when I did get married I would know what to do and how to do these sexual things nobody was going to teach me or talk to me about as a teen. These women were the standard-setters for feminine power and beauty to me. Maybe if I could store this knowledge away I would seem sexy and savvy to the men I'd eventually meet.

It's amazing, looking back, at how good I was at convincing myself of all those twisted things.

When conviction came I responded with "reason" and rationalization. I concluded that watching sex, and watching porn, couldn't be all that bad if the man I loved the most did it, seemingly without any repercussions. And it couldn't be all that bad if it was allowed on TV and in the movies. It couldn't be all that bad if it felt so good, physically. If "love" and sex were the main themes in all of the music I heard, obviously they weren't anything I needed to feel too convicted about.

Sex was for sale and completely mainstream.

But what I didn't realize was that my early exposure to pornography, without any timely conversation or education about purity, was devastating. It opened the floodgates of <u>sin-interest</u> in my heart and was my first real introduction to repressing and rationalizing soul-protecting conviction in order to satiate my flesh's interest and curiosity. It was where I first started to really practice and refine my techniques for rationalizing sin. Rather than understanding God's call to purity and responding to a holy anguish I felt from a heavenly Father who loved me, I instead ignored the tension God was pressing on me and welcomed a relief-bringing desensitization to sensitive things.

I wish I could say that my early exposure to pornography was the sole root of all of my sexual problems. Wouldn't that be easy? That might make the parents reading this book who believe their children haven't been exposed to porn yet let out a deep sigh of relief. We could all just blame porn as the one and only bad guy and point fingers and lodge complaints and then go back to not having to think too much about the overexposure issue, day-to-day.

But, in truth, my struggles with sexual desensitization weren't simply born out of my first glimpse at a graphic scene. They were born out of an <u>unguarded heart, unguarded eyes,</u> <u>and unspoken conversations that nobody thought to have with</u> <u>me.</u> They grew out of subtle, constant, and repeated exposure to broken, messy things and a lack of awareness that the entirety of what I was thoughtlessly *taking in*, on a day-to-day basis, was actually serving to significantly shape me.

It all starts mindlessly enough—I don't even think we realize how much we are seeing. I don't think we realize how slowly and methodically our brains are being conditioned by exposure to impure things.

We see less than half-dressed women in the magazines at the grocery store. We watch the funny and awkward sexual narrative play out between two dating coeds on the afternoon sitcom. There's the single bachelor and bachelorette stealing off for a night of romance on reality TV. Then the plot-essential, suggestive sex scene on the movie screen. We hear the song lyrics about the boy and the girl in the back of a pickup truck. The rap lyrics that essentially describe the act, thrust by thrust. We're flooded with Instagram bikini pics and news about the latest and most scandalous celebrity hookups and barely there fashions on models who look nothing like us.

We constantly see half-dressed or hardly dressed at all pics of anyone who wants to show off their body on social media. We scroll through the best of what young coeds have to offer on dating apps and social hookups. We click around to viral articles and megasites constantly pumped full of sexy images, barely there fashions, and permissive jokes about the millennial generation's "send nudes" anthem.

As preteens we're already in the midst of being awkwardly introduced to the budding hormones inside of us. All these things we are constantly seeing pique our interest and entertain us. They feel good. And look good. And please us. So why look away? Why think too much about what we're *taking in* if we believe the fact that we're not *putting out* is good enough? After all, we're kids. And all of this we're being exposed to becomes more and more normal, every day, to us.

Then gradually, over time, our interest is no longer piqued by the same degree of exposure and we pick up the intensity. And the half-dressed women in magazines become the completely naked women on our computer screens. And before too long the suggestive sex scenes in the movies become the hard-core porn in our browser history. And the single bachelor and bachelorette's night of romance becomes a trigger for our own arousal as we find ourselves celebrating and being entertained by the lust and drama of empty things.

Before we know it we've become young adults who moved from mindless kids to reckless teens because we were desensitized to the sensitivity of sex as a precious thing.

How did we get here? From innocent to unfazed so quickly? And, even worse, defensive about these things?

In a Fifty-Shades-of-Orange-Is-the-New-Kardashian world, there is no slowing things down. There is no way to shield ourselves completely from ever coming into contact with these things. We'd have to lock ourselves inside our homes and never turn on a phone or a computer or a TV. No, absolute avoidance isn't a possibility. And, in truth, shaking a fist at a lost world and trying to eliminate what's being pressure-pumped into the mainstream wouldn't be the first steps of correction anyway. Because completely changing those things is entirely too far out of our short-term reach. But what's not out of our reach is choosing, wisely and with self-control, what we see. After all, we may not be able to control what we are served, but we have complete control over what we choose to eat. word!

It is a basic principle, but a conversation that seems to have been forgotten spiritually. Or maybe a conversation too far delayed when we step back and look at the reality of the situation and the ages of exposure to certain things. We know that someone doesn't become obese after eating one cupcake; it takes long-term and continuous consumption of high-sugar, fatty foods. In the same light, we know someone doesn't become an expert in their field of study because they solved one equation correctly. It takes hours of study and practice and application to master a technique. And no one goes bankrupt from spending one dollar unwisely. It takes multiple poor decisions, irresponsible investments, or careless spending. And behind all of these things exist conscious mental choices and decision-making. So why would the same simple, guiding standard not be applicable to what we consume visually?

If you are what you eat, are you not also what you see?

Jesus spoke to this fundamental truth in Matthew 6:22–23 when He said, "Your eye is like a lamp that provides light for your body. When your eye is healthy, your whole body is filled with light. But when your eye is unhealthy, your whole body is filled with darkness. And if the light you think you have is actually darkness, how deep that darkness is!"

We are shaped by what we see. What we choose to watch. And what we consume, mindlessly. And spiritually, our clear vision of what God desires for our lives is blurred and blinded when our gaze is entertained by cheap and easy things.

We are what we see. And if the eye is the lamp of the body, then it is also the primary gateway for broken and impure things.

My early exposure to pornography and my constant, uncurbed sexual exposure from mainstream cultural outlets were gateway drugs into an addiction I never planned to battle. My eyes were the easiest opening for the enemy to pump temptation and fixation through, and my mind-set about sexual things was warped and framed by the world before the church even knew the conversations should be had.

Unchecked, and even permitted, visual overexposure robbed my sexual purity first, and it wasn't long until my rationalizations led my actions to follow suit. Think about this in parenting in future.

When What We See Becomes What We Do

The repercussions of visual sexual overexposure were like quiet cancers that first started growing within me. Women on TV and in movies, in magazines and pornography, became my measuring tools for sensuality and beauty. The world seemed to praise them as desirable and powerful, so they shaped my understanding of body ideals, worth, and sexuality. But when I looked at myself in the mirror I didn't see anything that looked like those women on the screens. I was a child so blinded by a false reality that I was comparing my young body to grown women's mature and often surgically modified bodies. I remember wrestling with deep (and illogical) feelings of inadequacy and insecurity as a result. I was talking to my poor mom and to my friends about my need for a boob job at eleven and twelve years old, already daydreaming about where I would go to get breast implants when I turned eighteen.

I obsessed over my weight, my size, my shape, and the aesthetic look of my body. Being a late bloomer—I grew seven inches in seventh grade and entered high school at six feet tall with an athletic build—already ostracized me from the flocks of young girls developing into their curvy bodies. Add on my deep-rooted, comparison-based insecurity, as well as other life factors that felt out of control at the time, and the enemy held my covetous heart's hand and led me into an eating disorder that was debilitating. All as a result of the cancer fostered in my spirit from an unguarded heart and unfiltered eyes. I didn't like what I saw when I looked at myself because it didn't seem good enough compared to the women my gaze was fixated on.

Not only did visual overexposure and a lack of understanding about what God thought about me, my worth, and my beauty lead to unrealistic comparison but they also led to a desire to emulate the things I saw and a dangerous desensitization toward my own sexual conduct. The character-cancer growing within me started to have outward symptomatic responses in my behavior and my willingness to compromise for things that were sexually tempting.

In an article fittingly titled, "What You See Is What You Do," the American Psychological Association notes that research shows that risk-glorifying media exposure is directly linked to more risky behavior. The effects are likely to occur both short- and long-term, while increased exposure is likely to be associated with increased risk-taking.[1]

In other words, it isn't just a seemingly uptight biblical belief that what we watch, listen to, and consume directly influences our spirits, our hearts, and our lives. It is a basic principle of human nature and cause-and-effect response. We aren't exempt from the allure, temptation, coercion, and influence of sexual exposure, no matter how self-righteous we claim to be in our ability to view certain things without having them influence our perceptions or actions.

I thought, for so long, that I was in control of what I was viewing and that it was permissible since it wasn't something I was actually doing.

Until it was.

Mark me down as another statistic, because my overexposure eventually led me right into risky promiscuity.

From everything I had seen, my mind had been conditioned to believe that part of becoming a woman meant knowing how to please a man. So my first real kiss was recklessly given away to a Swedish partygoer at a discotheque when I was traveling abroad for a soccer tournament at just age thirteen.

I don't think I even got his name. Apparently speaking the same language and even being able to say hi weren't requirements for handing over the first piece of my physical purity. Nervous kisses with local boys followed (you know, ones from the same continent), and more aggressive moves from some came in between. But just over one year passed from my first kiss before my desensitized heart sat in the front seat of a high school senior's Mustang GT. He had invited me on a "joy ride" and driven us back to an empty parking lot next to the construction site of an industrial building. The picture of romance, right? I was just fifteen. Naive and giddy to seemingly have a *man* who wanted me, I felt pressure to give more than I had before. And in that gravel parking lot I awkwardly tried my best to emulate some acts of foreplay I'd heard about from friends and seen the women do through those blurry channels on TV.

from the enemy. There was a sense of shame that bound me, but it was balanced by an unrighteous courage that grew in me. I knew the pleasure was shallow and the excitement was short-lived, but a part of me also felt "sexy." I craved the rush I felt when I learned I had the power to tease and please a man. I operated with a twisted perception of beauty and ultimately I liked that guys were excited when they discovered I was willing to do some of what they wanted, physically. It made me feel like a woman—at least more like the women I was constantly seeing. Throughout high school and especially into college, I eventually lost track of the number of guys who got a piece. But I convinced myself I was still virginal and blameless because I'd never given anyone *everything*. And by and large, the world's apathy toward purity and its overwhelming sexual appetite and influence supported that skewed theory.

Imprisoned by Pornography

They say the first step to finding healing is admitting we have a problem.

And Houston, we *have* a problem.

We don't just have a problem, we have an epidemic. A sin epidemic.

For the sake of perspective, let's disregard all other forms and degrees of less illicit sexualized exposure and simply look at the most perverse of all, pornography. Take away the sexual messaging we constantly hear in music, see on TV, watch in movies, see on billboards, are exposed to on social media, and any and all other avenues of visual influence we come across in an average week. Let's just look at porn. The most debasing and aggressive form of sexual imaging.

In the United States alone, 40 million people visit porn sites regularly.[2] I mentioned before that in one single calendar year people watched 4.6 billion hours of pornography *at just one website*. That is 524,000 years of porn—17,000 complete lifetimes. Just in 2016. Not only that, but across the board—among all demographics—one out of every five mobile phone searches is for pornography. Our most surface-level sin struggles here are an unbelievable issue with gluttony and idolatry.

And if we are fooling ourselves to think this is an issue just outside of the church—that somehow those following Christ are perfectly executing a profound ability to guard their eyes—then we are really out of touch with reality. The enemy uses this visual stranglehold in unbelievable ways within the church body. Among pastors, 51 percent admit that internet porn is a temptation. Not only that, but 64 percent of Christian men and 15 percent of Christian women admit to watching porn at least once a month. It can't be missed that the hearts lining the pews in our churches are human—just as apt to fall victim to visual sin temptation as anyone.

I think this is why, within the church, the conversation of porn and the overall topic of guarding our eyes as the lamps into our souls are often forgotten. Because it is a sin struggle that so many are fighting. And one that we have made so taboo, so cloaked in shame, so quickly judged that we've forgotten the compassion that would compel conversation about pornography. We've suppressed honest and real discussion because the enemy has convinced us we have no room to talk about it unless our eyes, hearts, lives, and track records are completely clean. We know, deep down, that we have suppressed so much conviction when we wrestled with these very things that we think our previous sins disqualify us from speaking. We grow paralyzed by fear of admitting we've fallen short in guarding our own eyes, and we forget that, by grace, God has called us redeemed. We are afraid to boast in our weaknesses and point to the power of the cross, so instead we stay silent and leave far too many hurting hearts feeling like they are the only ones weak enough to have given in to these broken things.

It's a shame, really. Because in failing to talk about the issue of pornography we are doubly failing to talk about the power the Holy Spirit possesses to purify our eyes, reclaim our hearts, and break our chains of bondage to visually perverse things.

A secondary struggle we are facing, framed by our silence, is that when the church does find the words and the courage and the angle to address porn, they are usually only talking to the boys about these things!

Can I be the first to stand on a mountaintop and scream, "WOMEN ARE STRUGGLING WITH THE EXACT SAME

THINGS!"? I think sometimes <u>the church tends to pretend</u> <u>that women aren't sexual beings</u>. Or, I should say, *as* sexual as males tend to be. Yes, the statistics are slightly lower when you look at the female demographic, but slightly lower is not at all synonymous with nonexistent. Or exempt from the need to have these things equally talked about, addressed, and taught. Maybe some girls are less sexually inclined by nature, but that was not the category I fell into. That was not at all my story. So I have to believe there are plenty of other women out there who may have struggled in the exact same way as I did. And plenty left equally as unequipped as I was in my wandering.

Currently 90 percent of males and 70 percent of females are exposed to pornography online in their lifetime. And based on increased accessibility and increasing market saturation, those percentages are steadily rising. Six out of ten teenage girls are exposed to pornography before the age of eighteen. And that isn't just simple, basic sexual imaging. That includes exposure to child porn, bestiality, sexual bondage, group sex, and same-sex pornographic scenes. Once girls are moving into young adulthood, 18 percent are using porn as often as once a week. And 18 percent of college women also admit to spending time online for internet sex every single week. I don't think it's the numbers, so much, that stun me. After all, I fell into every single one of those statistics and categories. I think the most heart-wrenching thing to swallow is another category I was lumped into: 49 percent of women who view porn deeply believe that it is a healthy way to express their sexuality.

Why is that so disturbing? Because I know, firsthand, how damaging that was to my own perspective of worth and beauty. Porn painted the picture of love and sexuality for me, as it does for many men and women.

But porn is not reality.

Our minds are being shaped by an artificial, heavily directed, sensationalized, and dehumanized form of sex that just isn't anything like real life. And not only that, our eyes are streaming in content that is framing an abuse-riddled model of controlling interactions in relationships. We are outlining our idea of power and sexuality around degradation, abuse, and false realities.

In pornographic films, 88 percent of scenes depict acts of physical aggression or violence, including rape, torture, and humiliation.[3] And 49 percent of scenes contain verbal aggression. Let's do some rough math here. If 4.6 billion hours of porn were consumed last year, and 88 percent of the scenes within those videos were depicting sex in a physically aggressive or violent manner, then human beings around the world allowed 4 billion, 48 million hours of violent, aggressive, and humiliating sex acts to stream into their eyes, their hearts, and their minds. And then they came back for more.

Carlo Scalisi, the owner of a pornographic production company, was quoted as saying, "Amateurs come across better on screen. Our customers feel that. Especially by women you can see it. They still feel strong pain."[4] In other words, this man was explaining that they like to use women in their videos who are new to the aggressive acts inflicted on them because it physically hurts their bodies more, and viewers really prefer to see authentic, genuine pain. In order for viewers to get turned on, they like seeing a woman authentically suffer.

That's where our sin-nature has led us.

The porn industry is linked to abuse on set, child exploitation, and even human trafficking. The same companies that are driving modern-day slavery, the sex-trafficking industry, are the ones who are profiting every time clicks navigate to and around a pornographic site. When we are viewing porn, we are a part of the epidemic. We are a silent financial partner in the booming business of human trafficking.

That's where we are led when we don't first guard our eyes.

While all of these statistics are disturbing, what they serve to do, ultimately, is paint the clearest and most overwhelming picture that the world, the media, the entertainment industry, and the porn industry do not care, whatsoever, about the integrity of what is set before our eyes. They aren't concerned with the state of our lives, our hearts, our bodies, or our purity.

But they like our money.

Movies, television, music, and other media waste no time in normalizing sex by portraying it as necessary, casual, unprotected, and consequence-free. They may slap ratings on certain things and say that it's the parents' responsibility to monitor what their children are viewing, but the entertainment industry ultimately doesn't care who sees what they are creating, as long as eyes are on their products, purchases are being made, and dollar bills are flowing in. Long before we are emotionally, socially, or intellectually ready, we are being inundated with sexual material as a side effect to the insatiable consumerism of a pandering world.[5]

The pornography industry generates around $13 billion each year. They love that they have found the formula to hook us. And they've capitalized on our brain's susceptibility toward addiction when some of its deepest fundamental needs can be stimulated visually.

You see, the reason "sex sells" in mainstream media and the reason the porn industry is thriving is because marketers, producers, investors, and corporations know the effect that dopamine release can have on the brain's wiring. Dopamine is a neurotransmitter—a chemical responsible for carrying signals between the nerve cells of the brain. It plays a lot of different complex roles in our brains, but one very powerful role it plays, to put it simply, is to reward us with a sense of euphoria—a "high"—when we are stimulated by something. It's the same chemical released when we cuddle a pet, eat a certain food we like, or hear a favorite song. While all these things are wonderful, what our brain really likes is the dopamine hits they provide. When dopamine is released, we are actually training ourselves, without realizing it, to want to repeat whatever it was that produced the rush.[6]

The good feeling is addictive.

We chase the high.

And every time we view something sexually stimulating, every time we watch porn, we get a dopamine rush that deeply, albeit temporarily, satisfies. Corporations know this—and also know that an addiction to what they are producing means a guaranteed income flow. They make money from hooking our brains and shaping our thoughts. They profit from our brains' dependence on keeping those pleasurable feelings flowing.

And as a result, we don't even realize how deeply we are being manipulated—how hijacked our brains and hearts have become. We are made puppets by strategic, sin-driven marketing that profits from the pleasure we become addicted to when we ignore any and all holy boundaries just to get the dopamine hits we want.

Why is so much perverse sexual material saturating our world? Why are the statistics of porn viewership so high? Because unguarded hearts and unguarded eyes are quickly corrupted. And where there is growing demand, there will always be thriving supply. Sexual stimulation is addictive, and the enemy knows it and capitalizes on it in the perversion of our society. But we don't have to be mindless pawns; we have the invitation to reclaim our eyes, hearts, and minds and to become queens seated next to the King on the chessboard of this life. We are what we see—if we're not careful, informed, and intentional in what we visually consume, the results can be devastating.

The most enlightening and accountability-bearing revelation we can make in the process of taking responsibility for our mindless consumption is understanding that sexual content and the sex industry as a whole are based purely on supply and demand. What we choose to set before our eyes and what we allow into our hearts and minds influences what continues to be set before our eyes time and time again.

One of the greatest by-products of beginning to become aware of what we are visually consuming is taking back ownership of our own lives. It's repossessing our health and the wiring of the very brains God has given us. It's personally reclaiming sex for the glory of God in our own worldview and understanding.

The world will promote a different message. It will sing a different tune. It will bring up every counterargument, every criticism, every opposing point of view to argue around the soul's deep need for monitoring, filtering, and guarding what type of content it consumes. There is no changing the hard-hearted trajectory of a sex-crazed culture fueled by big money. But I don't care how desperately the world tries to spin facts and figures to counter the thought that we are shaped by what we see. I know from my own life and from my personal testimony that what I was listening to, watching, being entertained by, and mindlessly consuming had a direct, devastating, and bondage-forming effect on me. The more I consumed visually, the more I was desensitized sexually. The more I used my right, freedom, and desire for visual fulfillment to rationalize my conviction, the riskier my behavior became. The more I thought I was competent and in control of the effects certain things were capable of having on me, the tighter the grip of the sin-braided rope around me. And as a result, even into college, porn was a massive struggle for me.

With New Eyes to See

For over a decade I silently wrestled with a fixation on pornography and sexual exposure. From eight to eighteen I quietly sought out and filled my eyes, my mind, and my heart with shameful things. All, remember, while flying my self-righteous banner of virginity. I learned to please my own body, sought out others to please it for me, and ultimately worshiped lust and lonely pleasure at the altar of shadowed and discrete anonymity.

Don't you know that's where the enemy likes us to suffer? Alone, in secret, feeling isolated, guilt-ridden, shamed. Juggling our rationalizations, stifling our conviction, and seeking fulfillment from anywhere other than at the foot of the cross that has the power to truly open our eyes and set us free.

I reached a place in my brokenness where it was taking more and more to feel the high I was desperately seeking. The porn I was viewing was becoming more graphic and perverse and soul-stealing. The things I needed to see were having to be more illicit for me to have any reaction or excited feeling.

Eventually I took to acting things out myself to get the rush of excitement and edification and affirmation I wanted from the guys I was seeing. Sending nude pics, video chatting, sexting. If you had told me then that one day I would admit these things in the pages of a book, I would have either fainted of shame or hidden my insecurity by laughing at how "prudish" you must be to think there was anything wrong with me freely expressing my sexuality.

But at the root, I knew the truth. I knew it was all empty. I knew it was all debasing. I knew it was temporary and unfulfilling and demoralizing. I felt void of actual love. Dehydrated of my confidence that I was worth much to any man without making sure he knew first that I was valuable sexually.

Porn had warped me. Life circumstances like my dad's suicide had emotionally wounded me. Promiscuity had plagued me. And I felt, ultimately, like I was wandering. Like navigating this whole maze of unfulfilling sexual experiences was as good as it was going to get for me.

What my eyes had taken in for years and years, my heart had translated into feelings of insufficiency and dependency on affirmation from others who were ultimately exposed to and consuming the same perspective-warping things.

But then Jesus collided with my story.

I wish I could fill these pages with the most detailed and vivid account of how God interrupted my life, stopped me in my tracks, and revealed Himself to me. But, in truth, I've already filled another book's pages with those things. So if you want to read details about the big-picture collision of my weary heart and Christ's wonderful mercy, you can pick up a copy of my first book, *Wreck My Life: Journeying from Broken to Bold.*

But at nineteen I met a King who stared right at my sexual brokenness, filth, and defiled body, and then picked up my heart and called me redeemed.

Jesus unveiled the *why* to me. All throughout Scripture we see Jesus traveling from town to town, place to place, having compassion on the afflicted, the sick, the lame, the suffering. And all throughout Scripture we see His love and mercy colliding with their faith in Him to bring about miraculous and life-changing healings.

The culture in which Jesus was carrying out His ministry and the culture we are living in now are vastly different in detail but unbelievably identical in the big picture. A culture plagued by unrealistic expectations and rigid rules of dos and don'ts enforced by religious leaders that motivated behavior modification rather than renewed and reverent hearts that longed to serve a loving God. And as a result, people were—and are—weighed down by sin-inclination, shame, guilt, desensitization, and ostracism. People pumped full of rules but robbed of guidance toward the greater *why* will always be dehydrated of love. And afflicted with desperation, addiction, and a lack of direction in their lives.

But what's beautiful is that "When [Jesus] saw the crowds, he had compassion on them because they were confused and helpless, like sheep without a shepherd" (Matt. 9:36). Jesus saw the desperation of impure hearts that didn't even know the depth of their own depravity and He was overwhelmed with compassionate pity. His love for them showed the deep mercy of God, and if that was Jesus's heart toward the people then, I must believe it remains His heart toward people now.

We are living in a society that is feeding off of our sin-inclinations, our easily addicted natures, and our naivety to the bigger picture of how we are supporting the very things that are destroying our hearts, our minds, and our bodies. We, the masses, are harassed by overexposure to sexual material. We are drowned in constant visual content that battles for allegiance and infatuation in our hearts. And we are blinded by all we see and all we are watching, all that muddies clear vision of God's desire for purity. We are sheep without a shepherd. Literally addicted to our lost wandering.

But even here Jesus meets us with compassion. His grace extends salvation to us and, in the same breath, refuses to leave us the same. The compassion of a God who sees us in our filth and washes us clean has the power to become perspective-shifting. Because when we invite the Holy Spirit to censor our lives and make sensitive our eyes, His response is vision changing.

you love us too much to leave us where you find us.

One afternoon I was sitting under the covers in my bed during some downtime between college soccer practice and class. Ever since Jesus had begun to change things in my heart, I had faithfully and repeatedly prayed a few things:

Lord, break my heart for what breaks Yours and bind my heart to Thee.

Give me eyes to see the world as You do. Give me ears to hear the cries of others and to love them as You do.

Give me wisdom to separate what is of the world and what is of You. Give me courage to walk in Your truth.

Lord, make me more like Jesus. Make me more like You.

I hadn't intentionally viewed any sexual material since the night God collided with my story and wrecked my life in the best way. But for whatever reason, that afternoon the temptation was strong and my mind was wandering and there were urges in my body I was growing tired of suppressing. I popped open my computer and clicked around to a familiar site that streamed pornography. And I will never forget the overwhelming feeling that overcame me the moment my eyes caught sight of a naked, pandering body.

It felt as nauseating as the first time eight-year-old me picked up that playing card by that silver pickup truck. My head was pulsing and my heart was burning and I couldn't close the computer screen fast enough. I sat there in shock for a moment as I felt hot tears well up behind my eyes. And for several minutes I lay there, alone, and cried. I cried and I cried. And I worked to swallow and process the shock of what had just overcome me.

I had prayed God would break my heart for what broke His. I had prayed He would give me eyes to see the world as He did. I had prayed He would give me wisdom to see the world as it was. I guess I was just overwhelmed that He had—and that the effect was all-consuming.

His reality

The sight of those pornographic images undid me.

My heart broke. My eyes ached. And I realized my soul had changed, drastically.

→ I think we are often scared to hand over our struggles because we're intimidated by the extent of the process we think will be necessary to work through things. But if I know the tiniest bit about how God tends to work, I know that His fierce compassion and our faith to believe He can break chains in our lives have the power, at times, to collide and bring instantaneous relief.

Romans 12:2 tells us to not "copy the behavior and customs of this world, but let God transform you into a new person by changing the way you think." The renewal of our minds. Then, we are assured, we will learn to know God's will for our lives, "which is good and pleasing and perfect."

I realize, looking back, that my prayers were inviting that very renewal without yet knowing this Scripture. Because as a decade-long porn viewer, I suddenly was incapable of looking at porn the same way. I immediately saw the women on the screens as daughters, as sisters, as fearfully and wonderfully made creations of a King. More than that, I saw them—for the first time—as human beings. Human beings whom God loved as fiercely as He loved me. Human beings who were trapped in sin and defiling circumstances. Human beings whom Jesus felt compassion for, just as He felt and extended compassion to me. And knowing the weight of the chains I had lived in, my heart broke for the internal affliction I knew those women were harboring.

I think one of the most detrimental effects of sexual over-exposure is that it ultimately changes the way we think about people. Far more than we even realize. Humans become objects and people become body parts. Individuals made in the image of a holy God ultimately become things to be used rather than people to be loved, valued, and seen. And when we come to a place where we are capable of dehumanizing others for our own sexual fulfillment and fixation, we're ultimately at the point of not only harming others but draining our own soul of vitality.

If we want to understand the root of where so many of our sexual issues grow, we'd be wise to begin paying attention to what we are seeing and watching and reading. Our awareness must shift to what we are taking in and what that's desensitizing us to. Our prayer must become, "God, give me eyes to see the world as You do." Because when we allow God to open our eyes to the realities of the world around us, we actually begin thinking about what we're consuming.

When the naked woman on your computer screen is finally seen as a daughter of the King who is being exploited for sexual reasons, your vision is renewed.

When the sex scene in the movie is finally seen as another cheap attempt for the box office to make money, your vision is renewed.

When you realize the reality TV show showing singles willing to compromise just about anything to get a rose and a ring looks nothing like a pure and holy and God-honoring reality . . . your vision is renewed.

But most notably, when you begin to see sexual things outside of the context of how God intended them—no matter the intensity or degree—as debilitating to your purity, you begin to understand why sexual sin breaks God's heart when it has such an easy and accessible stranglehold around us.

We are called, in Scripture, to guard our eyes and guard our hearts fiercely. May we have the commitment of David, who said, "I will set no worthless thing before my eyes" (Ps. 101:3 NASB).

If we are what we see, may we fight to reclaim our sight and fix our gaze on things that are true and holy.

IIIIi!IIII

Finally, believers, whatever is true, whatever is honorable and worthy of respect, whatever is right and confirmed by God's word, whatever is pure and wholesome, whatever is lovely and brings peace, whatever is admirable and of good repute; if there is any excellence, if there is anything worthy of praise, think continually on these things [center your mind on them, and implant them in your heart]. (Phil. 4:8 AMP)

5

Wandering for Worth

Do you believe you are worth what God says you are worth? NO. (11/30/20)

In chapter 2, we looked at our inherent value as human beings—as image-bearing creations of God.

But do you *actually* believe that about yourself? Do you *actually* believe your life, your body, your heart's purity are so valuable that they were worth dying for to redeem? NO.

Our honest answers to those questions sit at the root of most of our sexual sin. Because if we're being honest with ourselves, most all of us who have struggled in sexual sin would probably answer with a hushed, shame-filled, or defiant "no," for a whole host of reasons. The vast majority of us either (1) don't fully understand, (2) don't care, or (3) just don't believe what God says about us is true. And so, as a result, we turn to the world, time and time again, to assign us our value.

We mill around among the masses like cattle in a stockyard. Under the impression that we are just one of many—not particularly special, not particularly beautiful, not particularly any one thing that would make us worth much. In a world where everyone is desperately pining to be somebody, we eventually resolve to pine for the same thing. An identity.

But because we have missed, overlooked, or not weighed heavily enough what God Himself first says about us, we gradually become more and more desperate in our search for ourselves. We become more and more receptive to other people's impressions of us. And we become consumed with trying to present ourselves in a way that would somehow rank us high enough on humanity's twisted grading scale of "good enough." As if our lives depend on it, we become reliant on others to praise and affirm us—failing to realize the "others" we are relying on to assign our value are just as reliant on the same from us. And like livestock being hopelessly led to the slaughter, we willingly shuffle along to the death of our identity. With every step we take following the equally as insecure crowd around us, we lose ground on who God already said we were.

Our constant, subconscious, internal questions become, *Who am I? How much am I worth? How can I be better? Do more? Measure up?* We long for purpose, we strive for identity, we pimp ourselves out for a label we hope will define us. We think if we're skinnier or if we have better clothes, nicer possessions, or the best technology, then that will help us measure up. We want popularity, we want the best friend groups, we want the ideal relationship with that guy or that girl. Within the body of believers we even look at other Christians and covet what they have, the seeming depth of their faith walk, the Instagram-perfect life they project. We are certain others have it so much more together than we do. We are convinced others are more favored and blessed, are doing more important work for the kingdom, and surely are more valuable even in God's eyes. We are relentless dismantlers of our own self-worth. We evaluate, we rank, we categorize and subcategorize. We covet, we grow envious, we get competitive, and we harbor resentment. We want, we want, and we want. All because we've missed what we already have. We can't even celebrate others well, because we are clueless to and dehydrated of our own worth.

We end up wasting our lives constantly *comparing* rather than *repairing* our broken perceptions of ourselves. We don't believe, deep down, we are worth as much as God says we are worth. And we mindlessly consume the definition of value the world sells us, and the propagated message that we need to do more/be more/have more to be as good as the others around us.

But from comparison comes the need for affirmation. From the need for affirmation that isn't met comes a willingness to compromise in order to get the feedback we want. And from a willingness to compromise comes our desensitized ability to use our sexuality as a tool to get the attention we want. Since we long for an identity and are terrified of anonymity, we become willing to compromise anything for someone to tell us we're good enough. And the easy, repetitive, and addicting use of our sexual power to leverage the selfish need we have for an affirmation of our worth ends up tangling us, as well as others, in the stranglehold of sin patterns that eventually prove to own us.

Does that narrative sound familiar?

It's a pattern that is all too common among us.

Sexual sin is so easy to become consumed by because our sexual power is one of the easiest pawns we have to play. And if we never step back to assess why we are leveraging our sexuality in the first place, we miss the greater *why* in recognizing that it stems from an identity we have unknowingly misplaced.

Sex Appeal, False Freedom, and the Stumbling Block

It's really not hard to fall into the trap. If we don't know what God says about us in regard to our worth, if we don't know to guard our eyes and our hearts for the sake of purity, and if we don't understand there is a natural chain reaction through our sin-nature when one of these foundational needs for understanding is deficient in us, then it's not surprising when sexual sin wraps a stranglehold around us.

I can look back and so easily see all of the ways, through my youth, I was pining for worth and identity. And the first thing to be compromised in my hunt for affirmation was my modesty.

Long before I was sexually promiscuous, I was already learning how to use my body as a leveraging tool. The glances and stares that came from young guys excited me. I may have rolled my eyes at the honks and catcalls when I was out jogging, but, in truth, they did something for me. They affirmed me. And I enjoyed it. I liked when people noticed me. Even if all they were noticing was my body. I liked that, to whatever degree, they liked what they saw.

So, slowly, I showed them more.

Shorter shorts and skirts. Tighter shirts and low-rise jeans that "accidentally" showed my barely there panties every time I'd bend over. I enjoyed exciting the young guys at school. The guys loved it when the more popular girls flaunted and flirted with their bodies, so I followed suit to steal some glances. And the feedback I would get fueled my self-serving confidence.

Of course I used all of the surface-level excuses for the ways I would dress and compromise my modesty. Don't we all? We make the excuse that what we are wearing is what's in style. That the shorts and skirts only seem too short because our legs are so long. We point to the fashion trends and rationalize that everyone else is wearing certain things so we want to as well. We claim that what we are wearing is our personal style and our ability to express ourselves. If anyone challenges us, we get defensive over this, as if there are no other clothes on the market that we can find to express our style without being quite so revealing. Then, ultimately, we settle our argument by emphasizing that we can wear what we want, no matter who likes it, who approves, or who doesn't approve, because we have the freedom to do so.

At the root of it, you and I both know full well that there are deeper reasons we wear certain things. I liked feeling like I could captivate a man's mind. I enjoyed feeling desirable. I got pleasure from the attention it brought me. If I'm being extra-honest, deep down I wanted to one-up other girls too. Beauty became an attention competition to me. I liked when girls were jealous or even envious of the attention I received. I liked when I could mask my insecurity and instead wear something that made other girls around me insecure in their own bodies. We like the control games, ultimately. And our selfishness in enjoying and wanting the feedback goes so far as to twist into a willingness to cause others to stumble and struggle in response to the games we are playing.

But we would never admit this, would we?

We literally get so desperate to rationalize our deeper heart issue of wanting and needing affirmation that we leverage the argument of personal freedom to make ourselves feel better. Either forgetting or altogether ignoring that God, Himself, has spoken to that exact issue through Paul's letter to the Corinthians. "But you must be careful so that your freedom does not cause others with a weaker conscience to stumble" (1 Cor. 8:9).

Paul goes on to call out our excuses and speak truth. "You say, 'I am allowed to do anything'—but not everything is good for you. You say, 'I am allowed to do anything'—but not everything is beneficial. Don't be concerned for your own good but for the good of others" (10:23–24).

I remember when the deeper *why* behind my immodesty was first really challenged in my youth. It was a long time until my behavior began to actually change, but this memory never left me. It was always a compelling reminder of the bigger picture—mainly because it was so disturbing.

One of my best friends growing up was so very different than me. I think it's why I loved her so deeply. She was secure in who she was, wise and discerning in what she did, smart as a whip, and all-in-all highly unconcerned with how peers assessed her value. That's not to say she didn't care about what people thought—she was compassionate and kind and fiercely sensitive to others' needs. But she didn't let the world around her mold her, as a young teen. At least from what I saw and knew of her, she was confident, steady, and secure. A quiet and calm observer in a sea of cultural crazy.

I tried, on the outside, to seem like I was all of those same things, but she knew me. She knew I wore masks for the world, and because of her deep love she was always so thoughtful in how she talked with me. Sometimes a big ego masking a confused self-esteem needs gentleness and careful handling. And she carried my immature heart so kindly. It's funny; we can hear a message a thousand times over from a pastor in church or from a parent and never gain the wisdom being shared, but sometimes one grace-cloaked reaction or comment from a close friend has the power to change everything.

We went shopping at the mall one afternoon and I was in my standard teenage uniform—the shortest jean skirt I owned, a low-cut, skin-tight shirt that attempted to show off what miniscule cleavage I imagined I had, and an attitude and saunter I wore like perfume. As we walked along the upper level of shops I saw a group of older teenage guys gathered in a common area, leaning up against the railing. My friend noticed me as I spotted them and I'm sure laughed in her mind as my posture changed, my hips swayed, and I strolled past them flirtatiously. I looked back and watched their eyes stay glued to the bottom hem of my microskirt—I'm sure each hoping I'd take one stride too long and they'd catch a glimpse of something. I loved that they were staring.

Once we were a few stores away from the crowd my sweet and modest friend turned to me and rolled her eyes with a head-shaking half-smile—almost as if to reluctantly congratulate me on stealing those guys' glances and getting their attention. I knew they were probably picturing me naked and even thinking about having sex with me.

Mission accomplished, I thought. It was fun and fine to me if they imagined that, since they wouldn't actually be getting any action from me. I liked the power of being able to tease.

As a half-proud, half-kind-of-embarrassed shrug and sly smile crawled across my face, I caught my friend's eye as she then uncomfortably looked up and over at a bench we had just walked past. There was a man sitting there, probably in his late sixties, who had his eyes glued to my upper thighs and hemline too. And even though she didn't say much in that moment, it was so clear to my heart what her weary eyes were screaming. Sure, those young teens were lusting over my body . . . but that older man had been staring just as adamantly. And it was evident that he was likely picturing me naked and imagining having sex with me too.

I was so deeply disturbed when I made that connection that I hardly knew what to do.

I had the desired effect on people I wanted to, but I also had an effect on people I really didn't want to. Not only do we need to take responsibility for what our pining for approval is doing to the minds and hearts of others but we need to remember that we can't fully control our audience, either. When we compromise our modesty to exercise our freedom and wear what we want, we put ourselves on display for anyone and everyone—young men, old men, fathers, husbands—and we thoughtlessly encourage their lustful gazes.

In 1 Corinthians 8, Paul goes on to say that when we take up the argument of personal freedom and, as a result, sin against other believers by encouraging them to do something they believe is wrong or fall into sin themselves, then we are sinning against Christ Himself. If what we do or what we wear causes another believer to lust or struggle in purity, then out of love for others we should avoid doing it and wearing it. If we truly claim to be followers of Christ who love others and care for them, then our personal freedom should be less important to us than helping to strengthen the faith of our brothers or sisters in Christ.

You know, it's almost funny—we are often our own greatest handicaps. We sabotage ourselves, many times, in our pandering for worth and security. We desire affirmation so we compromise modesty in order to confuse and tease men's minds and gain their interest. In our impatient and insecure longing for love we are willing to give of ourselves so easily. We train men's minds that the pursuit is not necessary. We offer things easily and cause a chain reaction of others who will do the same to keep up and compete. Then we bemoan that there are "no good guys out there" because none choose to pursue us with patient expectation. We whine that there are no good men who know how to lead. And we fail to realize that we were first the stumbling blocks that hindered them from walking and growing in purity.

If we want to be respected, we must first respect ourselves. If we don't want to be a stumbling block for others, we must surrender our insecurity and not allow it to trip us up. How we dress, how we speak, how we act—they all serve as such clear indicators of our heart's health. Just as modesty and purity are by-products of security in knowing our worth, immodesty is a symptomatic response of a heart that is hurt. A heart that missed or never heard the truth that its life is worth so much more to a King who formed it first.

I think that's another layer of the conversation the church forgot—or struggles to handle with the right lens of focus, frequently. We, as believers, are often the biggest hypocrites. We promote the biblical call to modesty, and we talk a lot about loving others as Christ first loved us. But the church body seems to be the quickest to cast the first stone and shame any immodesty in someone who doesn't measure up. Don't get me wrong; issues with immodesty are rampant and seemingly out of control. It's hard to watch when we know what results. I am not at all condoning the standards of our culture—I understand holding fast to the standards of modesty and purity in a world that seems to regard them less and less. However, if we shame a girl who walks through the doors dressed inappropriately and forget to assess the deeper reasons *why* she may be using her body as a tool, are our hearts not just as impure in our lack of compassion and care? If we are the ones to whisper and gossip about our neighbor or peer or teammate who flaunts herself so freely, do we really look all that much like Christ? So many women in the world are hurting. So many are caught in the stranglehold of sin because they have never known or believed what God says they are worth. So many, including myself for much of my life, desire affirmation and attention to salve a deeper-rooted issue of not understanding their identity as an image-bearing creation of God.

We have to take responsibility for ourselves, love others well, and hold tight to Romans 14:10–13, which reminds us,

> So why do you condemn another believer? Why do you look down on another believer? Remember, we will all stand before the judgment seat of God. For the Scriptures say, "'As surely as I live,' says the LORD, 'every knee will bend to me, and every tongue will declare allegiance to God.'" Yes, each of us will give a personal account to God. So let's stop condemning each other. Decide instead to live in such a way that you will not cause another believer to stumble and fall.

I think it's time we put our pointing fingers of judgment and shame down, even the one we are holding toward ourselves in the mirror, and start to wrap our lives, our heads, and our hearts around the truth of what God says about us. When we take accountability for our own actions and understand the deeper root of where so many of our struggles begin, and are careful to walk mindful of others navigating the same temptations and deep-rooted needs, then we are better able to sacrificially love our neighbor. And when we learn, and share with others, how God sees us, it can't help but reframe our perspective of how we see ourselves, ultimately.

Dolce & Gabbana Girl

> You made all the delicate, inner parts of my body
> and knit me together in my mother's womb.
> Thank you for making me so wonderfully complex!
> Your workmanship is marvelous—how well I
> know it.
> You watched me as I was being formed in utter
> seclusion,
> as I was woven together in the dark of the womb.
> You saw me before I was born.
> Every day of my life was recorded in your book.
> Every moment was laid out
> before a single day had passed.
> How precious are your thoughts about me, O God.
> They cannot be numbered!
> I can't even count them;
> they outnumber the grains of sand!
> And when I wake up,
> you are still with me!

I love David's words in Psalm 139:13–18.
You were no accident. You were no mistake.

It doesn't matter your situation—the status or presence of your parents. It doesn't matter the words that have been spoken over you about your life, or the words you've assumed people have thought. It doesn't matter if you've been well loved or abandoned, cared for or cared less about, celebrated or separated from support. You were fearfully and wonderfully made *first*.

You were intentionally created by a God who knit you together in the womb of your mother. As a mom now myself, and a pregnant one as I write this, I truly believe that creation and formation are the most miraculous of all of God's works. What I mean by that is I have no idea how to grow a human being. If it was solely up to me, things would go horribly. I hardly understand adulting. Lord knows if I were responsible for properly creating this child it would somehow end up with tentacles and a beak. I have no idea how to sew personality and spirit into a child. I have no control over what features they will have, what will one day make them laugh, and what their tiny voice will sound like as they form words and sentences and thoughts that could impact the world around them. The details of my children have so little to do with me—and boy, am I grateful for that. No, I did not create them—God did. And let me attest in this moment, as I look into my firstborn's bright blue eyes and feel my second child rolling around within me, His works are marvelous. My soul knows that well.

You are God's handiwork. His greatest design. You were created with purpose—every day of your life recorded in His book long before your birth. You were planned, designed, tailored, and delighted in. You were placed where you are and with whom you are for such a time as this. You are God's masterpiece. And through Christ Jesus you have been created anew so you can do the good things He planned for you long ago. That's Ephesians 2:10—a verse that helped open my eyes to the ordained days of my life when I was blind to my own value and dignity.

Luke 12:6–7 so poetically reads, "What is the price of five sparrows—two copper coins? Yet God does not forget a single one of them. And the very hairs on your head are all numbered. So don't be afraid; you are more valuable to God than a whole flock of sparrows."

The God who formed you sees, knows, and loves His creations deeply. If Scripture in Genesis reminds us that we are the greatest of all of His creations, then what does that say about you? And how does that value reframe your perspective of yourself and influence the way you carry yourself in modesty too?

A friend of mine once taught on value through the simplest metaphor, and her words have always hung with me. She challenged the group of college-aged female athletes she was speaking with to identify whether they were a Walmart girl or a Dolce & Gabbana girl.

I think everyone's hands immediately went up when she asked who considered themselves a Walmart girl. Why? Because Wally World is cheap! It's an easy place to run and get what you need quickly; it markets itself around accessibility and convenience. Everything is marked with low, low prices, and if you've ever visited PeopleOfWalmart.com you know that you can walk in dressed in just about anything. (It's scary, really.) Anyone can shop at Walmart. The quality of the products is low, but Walmart functions on a first-come, first-serve basis where you can really get whatever you want or need for cheap. It's easy and appealing.

Dolce & Gabbana, on the other hand, operates completely differently. When my sister and I were younger, my mom used to occasionally set up day-dates where the girls in our family would all go to Phipps Plaza in Atlanta and spend the day enjoying the beauty of the designer stores, admiring the decorations in the building, and, by and large, daydreaming about how exquisite and fun it would be to be able to afford anything in the shops that lined the gleaming corridors. We couldn't afford a bit of it, of course. But there was something special to us about getting dressed in our best, making our way downtown, and just imagining.

One time when I was probably around thirteen I broke away from my mom and sister and made my way to the Gucci store to peek inside. The clothes and the jewelry and the bags were so beautiful to me. I was dressed in one of my nicest outfits and looked pulled together, so I thought maybe I could convince the store staff I was older and ask to try on a dress if they would let me. But as soon as I walked through the doors a security guard flanked me. Not because I was young or even suspicious, but simply because I was present in their store. The merchandise was so valuable they had someone assigned to watch every move of a shopper who would enter to make sure nothing was treated improperly. That caused me to act so carefully. I browsed, looked at an item or two, and even managed to try on a $3,000 dress, but I remember feeling, the entire time, like I was in a precious place. I needed to act properly, politely, and purposefully simply because of where I was. And because of the value I was among. Dolce & Gabbana is another high-end designer that functions the same way. So when asked to raise our hands if we were a Dolce & Gabbana girl, understandably among a bunch of college girls, there wasn't much movement in the room.

But then my friend began to break the metaphor down in regard to our spiritual worth, and it started to shift everything.

Why do we like Walmart? Because it is cheap, easy, and accessible. But do we carry ourselves like we are easy and accessible too? A Walmart girl has low value. A Walmart girl operates on a first-come, first-serve basis. If a man affirms her or makes her feel valuable in any way he is easily granted access to what she has to offer. He can come in any state of spiritual dress—there's no standard or requirement of him. A Walmart girl doesn't exercise discernment in who can come and get what they need. She carries herself like what she, as a woman, has to offer is cheap. And she resolves to give pieces of herself away recklessly. Low self-confidence and low self-worth are the banner of a Walmart girl.

But a Dolce & Gabbana girl carries herself differently. Self-confidence, humility, autonomy, and patience are marks of a D&G girl. Very few men even have the opportunity to shop at such a high-end store. It's first required of them that they present themselves in the best manner they have to offer. Clean and purehearted, with a well-cared-for soul. They are flanked by the guard and protection of the Holy Spirit when they draw near to her, She knows she is so valuable in God's sight that she's worthy of being carefully looked after. She's wise to guard her heart, for it's the wellspring of life. And because of that, only the spiritually rich are able to afford a one-of-a-kind Dolce & Gabbana girl. She is so incredibly valuable that only the men who have invested time and hard work into themselves, and learned surrender and stewardship in their walk with Christ, have permission to pursue her heart. Do you carry yourself as though you're a D&G girl? No, but I want to.

This isn't meant to be a materialistic teaching. I'm not saying you need to go out and buy designer things. But what I am saying is that you were designed by a King. And your body, heart, and dignity are worth valuing accordingly.

You are seen. You are known. You are purposed. You are loved.

When we can begin to root our identity and our worth in that truth, we can worry less about the value the world stamps on us. We know that same world's Creator has already defined us, and that should guide us away from needing constant affirmation and attention and praise. God sculpted you and wove you together down to the finest detail. Your body, your personality, your quirks—you were fearfully and wonderfully made.

What if we began carrying ourselves like we actually knew that to be true?

||||||||||

Charm is deceptive, and beauty does not last;
  but a woman who fears the LORD will be greatly
    praised. (Prov. 31:30)

6

In the Myth of Darkness

I didn't know he was married.

He was a friend of a friend and the restaurant's bartender and I was an underage college sophomore who was grateful he was willing to slide my friend and I the occasional cup.

I couldn't even tell you his name.

After all of these years, I couldn't even try to tell you what he looked like.

The details are as blurry as my discretion started to become that random evening our friend group decided we should go out to a local nightclub after our meal.

I vaguely remember someone mentioning in conversation that he had some issues and was separated, but at that point I assumed they meant divorced. I didn't really care, considering the fact that I wasn't interested in him and was confused why the bartender was even coming out with us. But I guess our timing coordinated with his shift ending, and a friend had asked him to join us.

The night blurred by and more tequila found its way into our cups. And after a few hours our whole group found our way back to my condo to continue hanging out and having fun.

He and I hardly spoke a word to one another the entire night, but somehow ended up in the kitchen alone together at one point. With alcohol in the equation, inhibitions faded, a lack of self-control, and a selfish mentality that, in the darkness, I could do what I wanted, one of us must have flirted with the other. Before I knew it we were kissing and, in my mind at the time, it was just a casual thing and he was just another guy who made me feel sexy.

The interaction was brief, as something distracted us and we drunkenly laughed and made our way back to the group, but the scars of that casual and catastrophic moment burned into me a deep wound.

I woke up the next morning, alone, with a hangover and a headache, and I stretched out in my bed mentally replaying the antics from the previous night. But when that foggy memory crept through my mind it stabbed my conscience like a knife to the gut.

Had I made out with a married man?

Had I kissed somebody's husband?

I tried so desperately to remember details from the night before. Was he actually married? Was he separated or divorced? How had we even been prompted to getting physical? How much had I had to drink? Had he and I even spoken at any point? Did anyone else see us? Did anyone know what we had done?

I felt horrific. Absolutely sick to my stomach.

My mind was spinning and my heart was pounding and I couldn't believe what I had done. I wanted, so badly, to know some of the answers to the questions reeling through my mind, but I couldn't stomach the thought of asking anyone.

If I brought up the situation and asked friends who had been at the get-together—and if no one would know about it unless I said something—then I would be humiliated and have to deal with unknown repercussions. I couldn't even remember his name, and the last thing I wanted was to be dragged into a situation between a possible husband and a wife I knew nothing about. In my cowardice, I couldn't bring myself to say a word. I pulled out every rationalization and excuse and shame-filled cop-out I could in my mind. No, this was too much . . . too big . . . too guilt-riddled. This one I wouldn't breathe a word about. This I would keep in the place I kept the rest of my sexual stories and secrets and sins.

This one would stay in the darkness.

IIIIiIIII

I wouldn't have been so capable of keeping this catastrophe hidden if I hadn't already been so conditioned to keeping all of my other sins in the dark.

I was an adulteress. I had, by ignorant involvement, been included in a man's act of infidelity. It didn't matter what the action was—if it had been a random, tipsy kiss or a premeditated one-night stand, in my gut I knew it was adultery. And never in my life did I imagine that this would be a part of my identity.

Yet somehow my soul was hardened and desensitized enough to press that truth down deep enough that I could pretend it wasn't as significant as it truly was.

Selfishly I tried to wipe my hands of the situation by villainizing him in my mind. By convincing myself that he and his possible wife were probably separated because he'd done this with other girls before. Or that it was his fault and his initiation, not mine, or that a young married man shouldn't be in the setting he was in with college coeds around to tempt him or be tempted by him. In order to ease my own angst and make it easier for me to keep this broken piece in the darkness, I mentally dismissed as much of the blame from myself as I could. I scoffed at the weight of his failures in order to try to diminish the severity of my own. I deflected responsibility from myself and, ultimately, moved forward disassociated from my sin. After all, isn't it always easier when we can separate ourselves from any personal accountability?

If nobody else knew, then I wouldn't have to answer to anyone about it. And for a sin this humiliating, the familiar darkness felt like a comfortable place to press my brokenness deep down into. After all, this pattern of mine wasn't anything new. Every sexual encounter I had experienced to that point had been carried out in the privacy of darkness too.

Perverting Privacy

It's dangerous, really. How appealing the darkness is. It feels enticing and permissive. It feels like something we're entitled to. It is a seductress that makes false but appealing promises and welcomes us in. It disguises itself as "privacy" because that feels warranted and deserved to us.

But in truth, darkness is a place beyond privacy. It's the very place we pervert the innocent right to privacy and twist it in order to serve the sin in us. It is our hiding place—a place where we unhinge moral absolutes and declare a right to secrecy, selective omission, and relativism as we write our own rules. The darkness only acts to serve *us*—our wants, our comfort, our egos and the sly sin within us.

We love to buy into the notion that, in the darkness, we can have our cake and eat it too. That we can do what we'd like free of judgment, with no one or nothing to answer to. That if we regret a choice or learn a hard lesson in the darkness we can still keep that moment there. Hidden. Detached from accountability or repercussions. Detached from anyone needing to know what we've been into. The darkness is like a siren that sings out all the things we want to hear. That we can hide our secrets there. That we are safe and have no reason to fear.

Our sinful hearts take the bait of those empty lies without hesitation. As millennials, especially, we are a generation that has somehow unfastened ourselves from the reality of accountability and responsibility and consequences for what we choose. We (really arrogantly) believe that we are above repercussions. In a consumer-centered, self-satisfying, permissive culture we have bought into the lie that we are free to make any and all choices we desire. And that if those choices are carried out in the darkness, we are exempt from being judged.

So the darkness is where we play. And everything in our culture reinforces that this is okay.

Our lust for sin and our shame-fueled need for secrecy around our sin create a hunger in us. The darkness whets our appetite, and before we know it part of our soul has made itself a home and filled its belly with the appeal of the enemy's lies of safety, shallow guarantees, and false security found in the shadows of reality.

So for me, at least, it began with abusing the privacy of having a personal phone and being able to text. Almost as soon as I was afforded that freedom as a young teen I abused it to serve the sin in me. Over time, flirty texts grew into raunchy exchanges that grew into sending pictures back and forth and having lewd conversations with boys over the phone.

The difference in simple privacy versus the darkness I was truly using it for—I was always terrified when my mom would punish me by taking my phone. I was always scared of what she may find or what type of message might come in. It's why the sinners in all of us breathed a collective sigh of relief the day that phones introduced the passcode security feature. It's why we triple-check to make sure we have the right recipient selected when we send our sex-fueled texts and pictures. It's why we can't let our devices out of a three-foot radius at any given time and why we panic if someone is looking at a picture in our photo album and, without permission, starts to scroll. Because we know we're in the wrong. We know it's all sin. We know we're ashamed. But we think that if we can keep it all in the darkness, if we can continue to satisfy our own flesh without having to be held accountable, then we can serve our wants without compromising our façade of morality to the people around us.

From phones it becomes the computer—the hidden and personal searches on the internet. Do you cringe at the thought of someone sifting through your browser history? Then you've probably got something to hide. And the storehouse of "private" things you consume in the darkness is probably sitting near max capacity. I used to love a locked bedroom door and an open computer screen. My ability to access whatever I wanted without being seen was so appealing. I reveled in the darkness of that perverted personal freedom. Anonymity is a coward's playground. And I never had to answer to anyone or anything.

It's in the darkness where our sexual deviance always plays out too. It's the parked cars, the back rows of the movie theaters, the college dorm rooms. It's the dark basements, behind locked doors, at homes when the parents or roommates are out of town. I once found myself climbing up through a fire escape onto an apartment building roof just to fool around with a guy. The only other person who would have known he was over would have been my roommate. But even still, I didn't want her to know about my business. So I sat on an industrial AC unit and gave pieces of myself away to a man who didn't matter and whom I had no ultimate interest in calling mine.

We become so accustomed to hiding it all in the darkness that repressing our conscience and convictions becomes second nature to us. Abused freedom compels us there. Shame compels us there. Guilt compels us there. And the deep desire for unsupervised autonomy, no matter how damaging, compels us there. Right into the darkness. Deeper and deeper and deeper we go until even the most demoralizing of sins can make themselves at home.

When we live as inhabitants of the darkness, we tend to surround ourselves with like-minded neighbors too. In an active and obedient walk with Christ, leadership, community, accountability, and discipleship are of paramount importance for the very purpose of counterbalancing our inherent urge to surround ourselves with others who will support our isolation in the darkness—others who want to feel better about themselves as they operate a good portion of their lives in the darkness too.

We are so heavily influenced by the community around us. We crave likeness and companionship. It's in our nature to gravitate toward those who resemble us. We draw especially near to those who justify our actions with unspoken permission. The ones who would never stand to challenge us or call us out and up.

Hurting people commune with hurting people. Dwellers in darkness find ease around others who "get it" and dwell in the darkness too. We don't want to be asked hard questions. We don't want to be challenged. We don't want to be held accountable. Ultimately, it's why, in the wake of my involvement with infidelity, I opted to stay mute.

Temptation, peer pressure, and the settings we put ourselves in are some of the most dominant catalysts for the sin we find ourselves in. In 1 Corinthians 15:33 we are reminded not to be deceived, that "bad company corrupts good character." But when we live a good percentage of our lives in the dark—and most, if not all, of our sexual lives in the darkness too—the bad company is exactly who we are drawn to.

The Elephant in the Room

We're only fooling ourselves though.

The sustainability of the darkness is just a myth.

No matter how skilled and practiced we are at keeping things hidden from sight, whatever is done in the darkness eventually comes to light. Luke 8:17 boldly reminds us, "For all that is secret will eventually be brought into the open, and everything that is concealed will be brought to light and made known to all."

In the reality of a God-designed, omnipotent-ruled universe, there is the gift of free will to choose for ourselves what we do, but there is no hiding sin.

God is not ignorant of what we tend to choose. He is not blind to where we attempt to hide our filth, nor is He vague on what the repercussions of our darkness-driven lifestyles stand to be without humility, repentance, and reverence for truth.

Galatians 5:19–21 doesn't mince words when it reminds us that,

> When you follow the desires of your sinful nature, the results are very clear: sexual immorality, impurity, lustful pleasures, idolatry, sorcery, hostility, quarreling, jealousy, outbursts of anger, selfish ambition, dissension, division, envy, drunkenness, wild parties, and other sins like these. Let me tell you again, as I have before, that anyone living that sort of life will not inherit the Kingdom of God.

We cannot afford to drink our culture's Kool-Aid and believe we are superior to an omnipotent and omnipresent King. Scripture reminds us, time and time again, the humbling truth of God's access to even the deepest depths of our darkened souls—after all, it is that very access that enables Him to reach deep into our self-dug pits and resuscitate our hardened hearts. We are only fooling ourselves if we truly believe the Creator of the universe does not have holy night vision in the most shadowed places of our stories.

The sobering reality of His saving mercy and His crushing judgment are painted clearly in His unchanging Word of Truth.

> So you see, the Lord knows how to rescue godly people from their trials, even while keeping the wicked under punishment until the day of final judgment. He is especially hard on those who follow their own twisted sexual desire, and who despise authority. These people are proud and arrogant, daring even to scoff at supernatural beings without so much as trembling. But the angels, who are far greater in power and strength, do not dare to bring from the Lord a charge of blasphemy against those supernatural beings. (2 Pet. 2:9–11)

Our self-empowered lack of fear of the Lord and His all-seeing, all-knowing power is what coaxes us into thinking the darkness even has any divine legitimacy. We may be able to hide certain things from the world for a while, but the assumption that we can hide things from God Himself is both presumptuous and soul-stealing.

Paul lays out reality in Romans 2:16. "And this is the message I proclaim—that the day is coming when God, through Christ Jesus, will judge everyone's secret life."

And he follows up that humbling truth with a word of warning that speaks right into our present wandering. "Don't be misled—you cannot mock the justice of God. You will always harvest what you plant. Those who live only to satisfy their own sinful nature will harvest decay and death from that sinful nature. But those who live to please the Spirit will harvest everlasting life from the Spirit" (Gal. 6:7–8).

The reality of our lives is that we are not alone.

There is an elephant in the room.

No matter how desperately we desire to live free of repercussions, conviction, and sin's weight, we cannot escape the accountability we owe to God Himself for how we carry ourselves as His creations.

The day this struck me the most powerfully I was curled up in sin with a boyfriend of mine at the time. We were alone, of course, in my apartment, and I will never forget the feeling that overcame me as we cuddled and things began to physically escalate. Like a wave of God's crushing presence I felt a sudden awareness flood over me that even though we were the only two people in my apartment, we were absolutely not alone.

I remember rolling over, turning my back toward my boyfriend, and staring at my closet door. In that moment I felt completely exposed—like Adam and Eve in the Garden of Eden when they realized they were naked and became completely ashamed. I felt, suddenly, like my ignorance was violating. Like my own arrogance was trespassing on my life, which was worth so much more than what I was enslaved to in that moment. I felt completely empty and completely consumed all at the same time. And when my boyfriend asked what was wrong I could hardly speak—I just remember asking him to go.

I'm so grateful for that day. I'm grateful for the courage I found to end that relationship a short while later, and the scales God was slowly beginning to pull back from my eyes. I was on the heels of sexual sin, but I was gaining awareness and my perspective was slowly beginning to shift toward some sense of holy reality.

No matter how hard we work to repress the truth, it does not change the fact that one day we will stand before the Lord and have to answer for even the deepest and darkest parts of our stories. And we will stand alone. Just as Ecclesiastes 12:13–14 says, we must "Fear God and obey his commands, for this is everyone's duty. God will judge us for everything we do, including every secret thing, whether good or bad."

Answering to God for all we have done is an unavoidable and assured encounter. But answering for what we have kept in the darkness can either occur the day we die, when our time to repent has expired, or be lived out right now while there is still an offer of light that has the power to obliterate darkness. That timing, even for a promiscuous, pompous adulterer like me, is solely dependent on our willingness to open our hearts to His truth and to fully surrender to His guidance. And that revelation, in my personal story, was abrupt and life-wrecking.

Somehow, in all the best and most unexpected ways, God broke through.

| | | | | | | | |

> O LORD, you have examined my heart
>   and know everything about me.
> You know when I sit down or stand up.
>   You know my thoughts even when I'm far away.
> You see me when I travel
>   and when I rest at home.
>   You know everything I do.
> You know what I am going to say
>   even before I say it, LORD.
> You go before me and follow me.
>   You place your hand of blessing on my head.
> Such knowledge is too wonderful for me,
>   too great for me to understand!
> I can never escape from your Spirit!
>   I can never get away from your presence!
> If I go up to heaven, you are there;
>   if I go down to the grave, you are there.
> If I ride the wings of the morning,
>   if I dwell by the farthest oceans,
> even there your hand will guide me,
>   and your strength will support me.
> I could ask the darkness to hide me
>   and the light around me to become night—
>   but even in darkness I cannot hide from you.
> To you the night shines as bright as day.
>   Darkness and light are the same to you. (Ps.
>   139:1–12)

7

From "Why Him?" to "Why? Him."

So much of our lives revolve around the "him," whoever he is. The boyfriend, the ex-boyfriend, the guy we like, the guy we hooked up with and were left disappointed by. So many of our emotions are dependent on the feedback and affirmation we get from him. From the excitement in the moments he cares about us to the heartbreak when he walks out or expresses interest in a different girl. Our hearts are escorted through life by the "hims." And we willingly give pieces of ourselves away to him. We're convinced we love him. Need him. Have the freedom to do what we want with him. And, ultimately, we put all our stock of loving and needing to be loved in him.

We thirst and we thirst and we thirst, always running back to the well for another bucket full of him.

But then the living water arrives.

He sits down by our well, points out our sin, and ultimately offers us the opportunity to never thirst again.

I love the story in John 4 of the woman at the well. How Jesus stepped right past what was appropriate or expected or in line with culture. He was a Jewish man, she a Samaritan woman. And her first response to Him encountering her was confusion about why He would even associate with her.

But He pressed on past her confusion and offered her spiritual fulfillment to quench the thirst in her heart and soul. He told her to go get her husband, and when she responded, in embarrassment and shame—with even more layers to her story hidden under her breath—that she had no husband, He continued to tell her all the details of her mess.

He knew she had no husband. He knew, in fact, that she had already gone through five. And that the man she was living with wasn't even one of them. In so many unspoken words He unfolded the layers of her hurt, her heart, and the shameful sexual banner that hung over her life. With so many unspoken words He looked this broken, immoral woman in the eyes . . . and still He sat by her well.

That's the same Jesus who steps past how shame defines our actions and sits down right next to our mess. That's the King who meets us in the throes of our dehydrated wandering and offers us living water. The same One who calls out every bit of our sexual sin, brings it all to the forefront of our minds, and rather than condemning us simply reminds us that handing it over to Him is what serves us best.

What I love most about the Samaritan woman who stood face-to-face with the One who intimately knew all of her mess is her response to what He knew and who He was. She didn't run away in pride or humiliation or guilt. She didn't hole up and take offense or retaliate. No, she realized He was who He said He was. She believed He was the Messiah—the One sent to save. And in response to His presence and love and altruism, she dropped everything and took off running into *evangelism*.

John 4:39–41 goes on to say, "Many Samaritans from the village believed in Jesus because the woman had said, 'He told me everything I ever did!' When they came out to see him, they begged him to stay in their village. So he stayed for two days, long enough for many more to hear his message and believe."

This is astounding to me. Especially right now in a world that when confronted with the truth of their sin responds with offense, anger, and rage. Here we see in Scripture, in the pages of this holy Word, that *because* Christ recognized and identified the sin in her, without her even having to say a word, many were amazed and came to faith that day.

Because God is all-knowing and still, in the face of our filth, remains—*that* is what should captivate our hearts. That is what should evoke our praise. Here is what this Word tells me, and what we must know to be true: not only do we have the power to be set free but we also have the power to be used by God, mightily.

This is a trustworthy saying, and everyone should accept it: "Christ Jesus came into the world to save sinners"—and I am the worst of them all. But God had mercy on me so that Christ Jesus could use me as a prime example of his great patience with even the worst sinners. Then others will realize that they, too, can believe in him and receive eternal life. All honor and glory to God forever and ever! He is the eternal

King, the unseen one who never dies; he alone is God. (1 Tim. 1:15–17)

That's the same Jesus I met.

He interrupted my life too.

Boldly. Radically. And abruptly.

He crashed right into my darkness, my pain, my circumstances, and my insecurities. He intersected my victim mentality. Collided with my promiscuity. Pummeled my pride and my arrogance and my suffering.

At my rock bottom—in the deepest place of my anguish and enslavement to sin—He found me. And His great love wrecked and redefined everything.

As I mentioned, you can read my first book, *Wreck My Life*, to access a deep and intimate look into my full testimony. In those pages you can read more of the whole story—the big picture—and all of the waves of struggle and adversity that were met with freedom and grace when Jesus interrupted my story.

My identity issues, my father's suicide, my depression, my anxiety. All of my crushing fears and insecurities and false realities came to a crashing halt—quite literally—when I challenged God to reveal Himself to me. And while there were other factors that compelled my desperate and burned-out cries, my sexual shame and exhaustion were paramount catalysts in my torment too.

I reached a point so dehydrated of hope and love that I wondered, at times, if life was even worth living anymore. I understood, in many ways, why my dad had put a gun to his heart and pulled the trigger. As scary as that seems. I wasn't the woman everyone believed I was. I wasn't the woman I even desired to be. And I didn't see a way out. I felt trapped by my circumstances and weighed down by my uncontrollable, yet unfulfilling, need for everyone else—especially men—to validate me.

It was terrifying. The weight and burden and bondage of sin has the power to blind us and lead us to places that are more demonic than we'd ever like to admit or believe. The thought of taking my own life wasn't foreign to me, and while there was other sin bondage that escorted me into those thoughts, sexual bondage was a dominant power player in that deadly cocktail of warped belief. The same sexual culture that our society treats as frivolous and fun and freeing. The familiar and even comfortable host that has the power to take us by the hand into dangerous places of suffering.

But God.

In the depths of my pit, God collided with me. Like He did for Paul on the road to Damascus, He literally stopped me, dropped me, and blinded me with His glory. For me the road to Damascus was an interstate between Baton Rouge and Atlanta, and He dropped me by allowing my car to wrap itself around a tree. But upside down, in that wreckage, God revealed Himself to me. And while I was hanging in my brokenness God downloaded the depths of the reality of the gospel of Jesus Christ into my heart. And I—a frustrated, exhausted, worn-out wanderer—ultimately came to believe.

Not because my guilt had caught up with me and I wanted to be a "better person." No, I came to believe that Jesus Christ was Lord because I was met by a Holy Spirit who opened my eyes to truly see my need. I was a sinner in need of a Savior. And in that car I was brought from death to life. My soul was resuscitated by mercy.

Mercy that opened my eyes to the reality of my sin and then gently whispered that, in Christ, I was redeemed.

The Humbling Reality

Step one for me was the personal recognition of my sin and my shortcomings.

I placed my faith in Jesus in that torn-up car on that November night because, really, there was no denying the non-negotiable reality of what I had experienced—of Who I had experienced—in that mangled Jeep. My soul was saved by God's amazing grace and by my faith to believe that He was who He said He was. But it wasn't long after the Holy Spirit filled my heart and refocused my sight that Christ Himself began doing hard but holy work in my heart and my mind.

One of the very first symptoms of my suffering He turned my attention toward was my sexual sin, the sexual narrative that had owned me for far too long.

God leads us to reckon with our sexual sin quickly because it holds such a different seat at the table in our lives. First Corinthians 6:18 clarifies that, "No other sin so clearly affects the body as this one does. For sexual immorality is a sin against your own body."

Sexual immorality is layered and complicated and self-harming. While all sin separates us equally from God the Father, sexual sin takes things a step further by separating us from humanity and dignity toward our own bodies too. It is one that not only divides us from God but also from ourselves as we voluntarily dismantle the very temple that houses and protects our heart. Sexual immorality unlocks the gates of our own fortress and freely allows plunderers and thieves in to take what is not theirs to own. And for those reasons, sexual immorality deeply grieves God's heart.

I would imagine it's hard for our heavenly Father to watch us willingly tear down our own bodies. I can only imagine what it would be like as a parent to watch my daughter give of her own body recklessly. So the first place He gently guided my eyes was toward taking responsibility, conquering my dismissive mentality, and humbling myself before Him with a heightened awareness of the sexual sin in me that He had sent His Son to die for.

That's where God leads us to begin: by first calling our reckless and self-satisfying behavior out for what it is—sin.

I will never forget the moment He delicately but unquestionably painted this reality onto my heart. Sure, I had grown up hearing all of these things—you're probably even tired of hearing me repeat them through these pages. But there was something different that occurred in my heart one night after I had come to know Christ and sat, eye-to-page, with a humbling Truth I now believed to be the unquestionable Word of God.

I was sitting in a faith-based gathering at a neighboring university in Louisiana waiting for the programming to start. Since I wasn't in my familiar stomping grounds, I didn't know too many people there and, as a true introvert at heart, I kept myself occupied by flipping through the pages of the Bible in my lap in hopes that people would think I was reading and wouldn't talk to me. I flipped to 1 Corinthians 6:9–10 and unexpectedly swallowed a heavy dose of holy but hard reality.

Don't you realize that those who do wrong will not inherit the Kingdom of God? Don't fool yourselves. Those who indulge in sexual sin, or who worship idols, or commit adultery, or are male prostitutes, or practice homosexuality, or are thieves, or greedy people, or drunkards, or are abusive, or cheat people— none of these will inherit the Kingdom of God.

I had been saved by grace, yes, but I hadn't acknowledged my specific sexual sin to God yet, and the weight of those words was almost crushing. I remember my heart pounding so hard it felt like it was going to edge its way through my ribs and out of my chest. I read and reread and reread them again and could hardly swallow the reality of where that left me. Wait, if I knew I was saved, but still indulged in these things, what did that mean for me? Was I actually saved or not? Was this Scripture saying that I, in my sin, was no different than someone wrestling with homosexuality? I was no different than those who openly worshiped idols? I was in likeness with a drunkard? An abusive cheater? Those people were such easy targets to throw the first stone at. But me? This applied to me?! In my unrepentant sexual sin—in the sin I was still kind of trying to hide from God and hoping He didn't see . . . in my sexual deviance and my struggles with porn and my promiscuity—this reality actually applied to me?

I racked my brain for a safety net of rationalizations and excuses that would exempt me from this reality, but the Holy Spirit within me wouldn't allow me to think my way out. I didn't know the theology behind these verses. I had no access to different preachers' or teachers' or biblical scholars' takes on the details of what these words meant in light of salvation. But, to this day, I'm so glad I didn't. Because the black-and-white words of God on that page were the simple, naked, and blunt truths my soul needed to see.

It wasn't about scrutinizing and unlayering and overassessing the context of those words. It was about humbling myself before the Lord, breathing in the truth that it was time to step away from my desperate need for justified reasoning, and simply believing the Truth—that there was no room in the kingdom of God for my self-satisfying justifications around impurity. I was a sinner—no matter which of those categories I fell into. We were all on level ground, no matter our struggles or bondage. I needed to repent of my sins and turn from my ways if I wanted to find rest and peace in the assuredness of my heavenly hope.

I love the Scripture that immediately follows those words I first saw that night. It reads, "Some of you were once like that. But you were cleansed; you were made holy; you were made right with God by calling on the name of the Lord Jesus Christ and by the Spirit of our God" (v. 11).

Those words met me with clarity. The details or varying extremity of my sexual sin didn't matter. What mattered was my willingness and humility to call on the name of the Lord Jesus Christ. And, in response, I would be redeemed.

That Love, Now Finally Found

That was the very day that my mentality shifted from "Why him?" to "Why? Him."

For me, the humble King who sat at my well offered me a love incomparable to what I had been chasing. When Jesus intersected the equation, He introduced immeasurable love and undeserved mercy. In every other religion you must earn your salvation. In every other religion your good works must add up to outweigh your sin and shame. Every other religion centers around humanity's ascension to God. But only in Christianity—in Christ, alone—is forgiveness offered as a gift of grace. Only in Christianity, in Christ alone, does God descend to us in order to make a way.

I was the adulterer to be stoned. And even still, His love found me.

I couldn't help but think of all I had kept in the darkness when I came across John 8, the story of the woman caught in adultery and brought to Jesus. I couldn't help but think of that drunken moment with an unfaithful man in the confines of that kitchen. But when I read verses 3–11, my soul was even further captivated by the One who said He loved me.

As he was speaking, the teachers of religious law and the Pharisees brought a woman who had been caught in the act of adultery. They put her in front of the crowd.

"Teacher," they said to Jesus, "this woman was caught in the act of adultery. The law of Moses says to stone her. What do you say?"

They were trying to trap him into saying something they could use against him, but Jesus stooped down and wrote in the dust with his finger. They kept demanding an answer, so he stood up again and said, "All right, but let the one who has never sinned throw the first stone!" Then he stooped down again and wrote in the dust.

When the accusers heard this, they slipped away one by one, beginning with the oldest, until only Jesus was left in the middle of the crowd with the woman. Then Jesus stood up again and said to the woman, "Where are your accusers? Didn't even one of them condemn you?"

"No, Lord," she said.

And Jesus said, "Neither do I. Go and sin no more."

When I acknowledged my sexual sin for what it was, took accountability for my actions and my choices, and brought my sin to the throne of grace, I collided with the love I had always desired. The love I had spent my life seeking. Jesus entered my sexual testimony, and His great love changed everything.

That was the greatest and most heart-transforming part of my equation.

When "Why him?" transformed into "Why? Him."

It was the most compelling *why*.

Because it's at the foot of the cross that our sin and God's grace collide. And He doesn't meet us with condemnation and rage—He loves us and instructs us to go and sin no more.

"But God showed his great love for us by sending Christ to die for us while we were still sinners" (Rom. 5:8). That love and sacrifice carry a perspective-shifting weight. God doesn't desire for us to live in our shame or humiliation or chains. He's not pointing fingers and casting blame. Our sexual sin struggles have already been paid for. The path has already been paved for us to be forgiven and redeemed. The question is, do we truly believe?

If we choose to believe that Jesus's life and death meant something—no, not just something . . . everything—in our lives, then we are forgiven of our sins and offered new life. And that exchange, that holy and unprecedented salvation, is the compelling root at the base of our life-change.

The remedy for our sexual sin problem is not behavior modification, it's heart transformation. God, through Christ alone, is the one place we can find the power for true heart transformation in our lives. When we're in sexual sin, it's not enough to say that we know we need to *not* want to sin. We're always going to want it. What must happen is that our *want* to honor God and surrender ourselves in gratitude for His incredible love for us must become greater than our want of sex outside of His design. The "not" will never come. But the greater want can be cultivated in a willing heart. When we grasp that what was done at the cross for us can compel a genuine response of gratefulness and love, we regain control of our desires in a holy capacity.

That saving love is the catalyst of our obedience to God's design for our lives. It's what makes the Word of God matter. It's what makes His instruction and commissioning carry any type of weight. It's what helps us swallow the fact that we are in sin and humbly admit that we need forgiveness—even when it hurts. Even when it's hard. Even when it makes no sense whatsoever at the time.

His great love for us is the greatest root of the *why*.

And that love can't be trivialized.

Because that *hope* we find when we lay down our sin at the cross and learn we are set free of its life-stealing cost—that hope is what changes everything. It is what compels us to actually care about what God has to say about our worth, our bodies, and our sexual decision-making.

When I collided with that hope and love, it finally began to transform things within me. I knew His unfailing love toward those who fear Him was as great as the height of the heavens above the earth. He had removed my sins as far "as the east is from the west" (Ps. 103:11–12). My old sinful self was crucified with Christ so that sin might lose its power in my life. I was no longer a slave to sin. For when I died with Christ I was "set free from the power of sin" (Rom. 6:6–7).

Because of that love, my interest in the world was crucified. I was being transformed into a new creation and the only thing I cared to chase after from that point forward was the cross of Jesus Christ.

I knew that any boy could undress me and make me feel like a queen for a night, but it was going to take a *man* to help armor me up and point me to the King of my life. As far as I could tell, there were no men like that to be found. So in response to God's great love for me, I knew I needed to take a season of intentional time to lay my life down.

IIIIıIIII

But God is so rich in mercy, and he loved us so much, that even though we were dead because of our sins, he gave us life when he raised Christ from the dead. (It is only by God's grace that you have been saved!) For he raised us from the dead along with Christ and seated us with him in the heavenly realms because we are united with Christ Jesus. So God can point to us in all future ages as examples of the incredible wealth of his grace and kindness toward us, as shown in all he has done for us who are united with Christ Jesus. God saved you by his grace when you believed. And you can't take credit for this; it is a gift from God. (Eph. 2:4–8)

8

Participating in the Healing

Do you know what I love about the story of the prodigal son? Even though I can most closely relate to the younger son— the one who neglected his blessings, ran from accountability, squandered his life, and indulged in all that sin had to offer until, ultimately, he was left with nothing and wearily made his way back home—he isn't the most notable character in the story to me. The story isn't even most significant to me because of the older brother—the one who was obedient, careful, faithful, and disciplined in how he carried his blessings. No, I love the narrative because of the father. He is the most noteworthy person in the story. Because the father was the one who was wronged. The father was the one who loved his son, then watched as his son threw it all back in his face. The father was the one who likely sat up, heart-wrenched, through the long and dark nights of his son's wandering. The father was the one whose very gifts were being wasted and squandered and gambled away to sinful things. The father was the one who had every right to be mad, resentful, offended, and anger-filled when he caught sight of his son returning home empty-handed, off in the distance.

But the *father* is the one who went running!

At the first sight of his son the father dropped everything and ran out to meet him. He embraced him, his heart of love poured out over him, and he celebrated in response to the sinner's return home.

The father is the picture of God's great love. I still to this day stand in awe of that grace and hope.

That kind of love compels something in us. It is a radical love that warrants a response. The fact that God, Himself, joyfully welcomes us back—that type of love is too great, too pure, too merciful an act. In my life, that love stopped me in my tracks.

> The temptations in your life are no different from what others experience. And God is faithful. He will not allow the temptation to be more than you can stand. When you are tempted, he will show you a way out so that you can endure. (1 Cor. 10:13)

I was comforted in hearing these words because they (1) lifted the weight of feeling like I had been too weak or too misguided to be eligible for grace, and (2) reminded me that God was with me and for me—completely capable of guiding me out of my bondage and shame, by His wisdom and strength.

It didn't take long after coming to know Christ and coming to grips with the reality of my sexual sin for me to realize it was going to have to be an enormous effort on my part to surrender my wants and urges over to Him. For far too long I had given men my body in hopes that they would give me their hearts. I had spent too long in the darkness, too long filling my ears and eyes with things I didn't need to hear or see. I had wasted too much time being enslaved to my sin, enslaved to my lusts, and enslaved to my insecurities. There were very real, very dominant, very debilitating things that needed to die in me. And I knew, deep in my spirit, that breaking those chains was going to require incredible intentionality. I was going to have to fight like hell against my flesh and against the enemy. But I finally knew and truly believed God, in His rich love and mercy, was willing to and capable of making a way for me. I was finally coming to understand that it wasn't about my behavior changing first in order to be "good enough" but rather it was about my heart condition being radically shifted. My actions and behaviors would change as an overflow of response compelled by that incredible and undeserved grace.

Fasting from Intimacy

We'd idealistically like to believe that we can simply pray for something and God will carry out our wishes immediately. Especially when they are righteous, God-honoring prayers. We would like to think that if we prayed for patience we could wake up the next morning more patient beings. That if we prayed for self-control certainly we could immediately be granted more restraint and discernment. We would like to think that if we pray for healing we could snap our fingers and be whole and complete. And while immediate miracles certainly aren't out of God's wheelhouse of possibility, I've found that His responses are not necessarily instantaneous. More times than not, He actually opts to grow our character and faithfulness by inviting us into the healing.

When we pray for patience, God usually gives us *opportunities* to practice patience—no matter how taxing. When we pray for self-control, God usually presents *opportunities* where dependence on the Spirit and denial of self can grow us. When we pray for healing God usually grants us *opportunities* to learn more about His nature and grow more in wisdom and humility as we are invited into the process of healing. It is the training, the process, the daily walk that challenges, stretches, and strengthens us. It is the focus and faith and trust in the patient, purposeful steps that make us battle-ready.

So while I wished I could have simply prayed that God take all of my shame, all of my guilt, all of my habits, and all of my dependencies away immediately, the truth was that there was hard but holy heart-work that needed to be done in me. While instantaneous answers are usually most appealing, stripping back the layers of my sexual oppression was going to take time and purposeful surrender. Scripture calls us to act in response to God's mercy. To crucify the flesh, to nail our passions and desires to the cross, to live by the Spirit's leading, and to walk in step with the Spirit in every area of our lives (Gal. 5:24–25). I needed to act in ways that intentionally steered me clear from stumbling blocks and made room in my cluttered heart for God to do the necessary work in me.

He confronted me with it—a proposition to my spirit that would give God the time and space to get through to my calloused and scabbed heart.

A year-long intimacy fast.

That He desired I immediately start.

I resisted it. I pushed back against it. I wanted patience and self-control and healing, but I didn't know it would require such an expense. I tried to suppress the prompting, tried to rationalize the inconvenience, tried to bargain my way around to a different means of healing. But I'll never forget the words God so poetically strung through my heart:

I love you. I am jealous for you. I want to be the relationship you fully choose.

You are Mine and I am yours. I long to be your Bridegroom.

But a monogamous relationship with Me can never be sustained if you cave to the whims of an adulterous heart.

So for a year I want you to delight in Me. I long for all of your heart.

I couldn't help but be flooded by the black-and-white, raw-and-real, heart-shaping words that Jesus so simply but so intentionally spoke in Matthew 22:37–39. "'Love the Lord your God with *all* your heart and with *all* your soul and with *all* your mind.' This is the first and greatest commandment. And the second is like it: 'Love your neighbor as yourself'" (NIV, emphasis added).

The collision of this Scripture's call and the words God had braided through my soul made up my mind for me. As nervous and anxious as I was about handing over a year of my life, I stepped into the challenge hopefully. I committed to a year of intimacy exclusively with Jesus and decided to carry myself as if I were taken. I didn't allow my eyes to wander, I didn't flirt, and I didn't give a bit of myself away physically. I entered into a yearlong commitment of divine monogamy, which I dubbed "Kissless Till Next Christmas," and never could have imagined all God was going to heal in me.

||||||||||

We live in a culture that scoffs at singleness. We almost treat it like a disease. But can I just be the first to stand up and scream that singleness is *amazing*? I say that as a happily married woman with children who is grateful for the season of life I'm currently in. But man, looking back, when I reflect on my intimacy fast and my one-on-one time with Christ, alone . . . it was everything.

Not only did God use every day, every week, every month of that journey to open my eyes and my heart to incredible and revelatory truths and realizations and teachings, but He also used that season of my life to powerfully and decisively utilize me for kingdom work He was orchestrating.

It was an absolute battlefield to step away from so many things I had deeply depended on for so much of my life, but God used every second of that time to fill me. He encountered me with truths about my worth, my value, my identity, and my security. He equipped me with strength, with focus, with wisdom, and with clarity. He taught me how to daily walk with the Spirit. His love compelled me to begin opening my Bible and filling my heart and mind with the Truth of the Word. He escorted me into a beautiful and multifaceted prayer life. He daily empowered me to courageously and boldly flee from sin. He comforted me as my obedience to Him separated me from people who didn't understand and were judgmental of my new choices. He coached me in how to take my thoughts captive and surrender them to Him— every time I had the urge to pleasure myself, every time I had the urge to dive into sin through my computer screen, every time I had the urge to seek affirmation and worth from old flings I would bump into or get texts or calls from when they had sexual needs. No, in the face of sexual sin, He grew unwavering confidence in me that I could call upon Him and He would meet my every need.

> I prayed to the LORD, and he answered me.
>   He freed me from all my fears.
> Those who look to him for help will be radiant with
>   joy;
>   no shadow of shame will darken their faces.
> In my desperation I prayed, and the LORD listened;
>   he saved me from all my troubles.
> For the angel of the LORD is a guard;
>   he surrounds and defends all who fear him. (Ps.
>   34:4–7)

But above all else, in that season of singleness and surrendered intimacy, He unexpectedly and powerfully invited me into the process of participating in my own healing.

The Prostitute Who Broke My Heart

It wasn't that I had never visited a slum within a lesser developed country before—the bruises that the slums of Kampala, Uganda, had left on my heart from an earlier mission trip were still healing. But walking through the slums of La Carpio in Costa Rica was different. Not because the conditions were any better or worse compared to Africa, but because the condition of my heart was different. For better and for worse, my heart had changed.

I had been moving through my intimacy fast for months and months. I had experienced significant healing and growth and spiritual maturity in that time, but there was still work in my heart that needed to be done. I couldn't identify exactly what it was, but I could sense myself getting complacent and even a bit self-righteous in how far I had come. But my healing was ongoing, and God used a prostitute in the streets of Central America to help me realize there was still some heavy lifting to be done.

After navigating through the streets of La Carpio—a slum community comprised of 44,000 people, 30,000 of which are children, that literally sits in the center of the city's landfill—we found our way to the Methodist church we were partnering with for the day. Stepping over streams of human waste, reading gang insignia painted across shanty huts, and watching hungry children litter the streets alongside hungry cats and dogs served a heavy blow to my heart. But I worked to keep my composure and focus on the day's tasks.

We started by helping to fill plates and bellies through the church's weekly feeding program. The laughter and chatter moved to the back of the building as we wrestled and danced with beautiful, brown-eyed babies for hours on end. We tried to lead the kids through a few Bible school songs and stories, but quickly found that more than they needed education in that moment, they just needed attention. A friend to laugh with, a "gringo" to climb on, a pair of eyes to look into theirs and care. Truly care. They were thirsty for love, and so we loved as deeply as time allowed.

As the children danced out of the church and scattered throughout the clutter and grime of the neighborhood, the pastor's wife gathered us to talk. Through a translator, she shared a powerful message of faith and belief. Belief in all things good. Belief in love and restoration and provision. Belief in perseverance—even when hope was hard to find. As she talked, we wept. As she wept, we prayed. And as the sun began to lower over the garbage-littered outskirts of La Carpio, we worshiped.

But as we prayed and sang, I found my mind in a far different place. I felt guilty for a moment that I wasn't able to fully focus my prayers on the depravity around me but I quickly began to realize that God was prompting me to pray, first, for the depravity still in my own heart.

I arrogantly resisted for a few minutes—the pride of my own mind holding me back. I sat on my knees in a state of stubborn, spiritual complacency and argued with God that my heart was fine. That the issues in these slums were far more pressing than the issues of my heart and of my sexual past I was processing through. After all, I was the missionary here. I was the one who had plenty, while these people had nothing.

And with all the ease and might of a perfectly loving God, He simply pressed a bone-trembling truth on my heart:

You are no more free of bondage than the prostitute who sits outside the door, if you have not love.

I opened my eyes and peered through the dirty concrete opening we had entered in through. Just outside of the church sat a young girl, no older than fifteen. Her hair was combed and shining. Her clothes were clean and pressed. Her makeup was perfectly applied to her gentle skin. And there she sat. Alone. Leaning against the corner of a shanty, her feet propped over the stream of sewage that ran underneath her. And there she waited in hopelessness. There she waited for someone to come along and give her worth.

A hot tear boiled in my eye and before I could even collect my thoughts, God began to lay a list of names on my heart. A list of names I had buried so deep. A list of names I was sure I was beyond at that point in my healing. A list of names I had tried to distance myself from for so long.

But one by one, God began to whisper the specific names of men I had physically given pieces of myself away to in the past. Name after name after name He whispered. Name after name after name. Before I knew the words my lips were forming, I realized I was praying for each of those men by name. As He so gently reminded me of each indiscretion, I lifted each person up. I prayed for the salvation of some, the forgiveness of others, the health and growth of the rest. Name after name after name.

As I prayed, I realized a wrecking truth: I had never once prayed for a single one of these men before. My wild years were behind me and I had processed through my own failures months earlier. But I had never truly forgiven those men. I had never even brought their names before God. I had only loved myself enough to erase the memories. I had never loved others enough to genuinely let myself care.

You are no more free of bondage than the prostitute who sits outside the door, if you have not love.

Love. Forgiveness. Compassion. I desired, so deeply, all of these things in that moment. I looked at that beautiful girl and saw how God sees all of us in our sexual sin. Beloved children trapped among the slums of our own pride. Just as my heart broke for that prostitute, His heart breaks for us when we sit in unforgiveness. Full and complete healing can never happen if we haven't sought forgiveness and received forgiveness, fully.

If I could speak all the languages of earth and of angels, but didn't love others, I would only be a noisy gong or a clanging cymbal. If I had the gift of prophecy, and if I understood all of God's secret plans and possessed all knowledge, and if I had such faith that I could move mountains, but didn't love others,

I would be nothing. If I gave everything I have to the poor and even sacrificed my body, I could boast about it; but if I didn't love others, I would have gained nothing. (1 Cor. 13:1–3)

If I wanted to experience healing, I had to genuinely love the men who had sinned against me and the men I had roped into my sinning. Dragging the skeletons from my closet was in no way comfortable but it was necessary. I couldn't keep unforgiveness hidden.

I would argue it's the most painful part, but it's how God invites us to participate in our own healing. Soul ties are formed with others when we are sexually involved. The intent of sex is to unify two into one. When we are sexually deviant outside of marriage we are left vacant and ensnared, because sex unites you and then the lack of covenantal commitment tears you apart. But the tears are never clean; there are always scraps left in the ripping. And soul ties can linger even in the most sorry heart. The only way soul ties are broken is through the catastrophic power of the cross—the most complete picture of forgiveness. God invites us into our own healing with the invitation to extend forgiveness and ask to be forgiven ourselves.

In Jesus's Sermon on the Mount he speaks to this very principle:

You have heard that our ancestors were told, "You must not murder. If you commit murder, you are subject to judgment." But I say, if you are even angry with someone, you are subject to judgment! If you call someone an idiot, you are in danger of being brought before the court. And if you curse someone, you are in danger of the fires of hell. So if you are presenting a sacrifice at the altar in the Temple and you suddenly remember that someone has something against you, leave your sacrifice there at the altar. Go and be reconciled to that person. Then come and offer your sacrifice to God. (Matt. 5:21–24)

It seems crazy. But it is a model that compels us to look a little more like Jesus. Who are we to withhold forgiveness from another when God Himself withholds no forgiveness from us? Hoping to be healed but opting not to forgive another is like drinking poison and hoping the other person will die. It is not the other person who is afflicted by unresolved issues. It is the very core of our own hearts.

It was embarrassing at first, but ultimately liberating, as I made my way home and began reaching out to guy after guy I had involved myself with. I sent texts and Facebook messages in the weeks that followed. For the ones whose names I couldn't remember—because of how much time had passed or because of my state of intoxication when we were involved—I simply brought their faces to God in prayer; after all, He knew their names and their souls. Some men laughed, some men scoffed, and some didn't quite know what to say. But others were genuinely grateful and, with a few, it opened up conversation that was ultimately glorifying to this God I was coming to know, this God of immeasurable grace.

The final step of forgiveness God drew me to was to my own personal, full acceptance of His forgiveness for the things I had chosen to do. I had to push past my shame, guilt, and doubt that God's grace was sufficient for me. Proverbs 4:23 reminds us to guard our hearts above all else, for our hearts determine the course of our lives. And, in truth, we can sometimes be the fiercest inflicter of our heart's own wounds. I had to reckon with myself, bury my pride, and willingly accept that Christ's life, death, and resurrection were sufficient for me to die to my shame and be made completely and boldly new in God's eyes. The truth was, I really could be freed from the bondage of sin. "So if the Son sets you free, you are truly free" (John 8:36). But I had to accept, receive, and believe that to be true in my own life too.

The Faith to Believe

Time and time again, in Scripture, we see healing happen because the person who desired healing, or the person who came on behalf of an ill individual, truly and wholeheartedly had the faith to believe they would be healed. Over and over and over again we see this narrative play out in Jesus's ministry. And, in response to those healings, we see the believers compelled to worship, praise, and respond.

I love the retelling in the Gospels of one of Jesus's many miracles—healing Peter's mother-in-law.

> After Jesus left the synagogue with James and John, they went to Simon and Andrew's home. Now Simon's mother-in-law was sick in bed with a high fever. They told Jesus about her right away. So he went to her bedside, took her by the hand, and helped her sit up. Then the fever left her, and she prepared a meal for them. (Mark 1:29–31)

Like, what? What a sight that would have been to see. And what a compelling picture of what our lives should look like when we have the faith to believe He is capable of setting us free. When He does, would we be compelled to surrender and serve like the mother of Peter's wife? She didn't even hesitate to humble herself—the fever left her and she got up to prepare a meal. Jesus healed her and she immediately got up to lay down her life.

There is immeasurable beauty in participating in our own healing. There is incomparable wonder in taking up our cross and laying down our lives. God desires freedom for us but He never neglects the opportunity to teach us, grow us, and welcome us into the journey of being refined. It may be hard, it may be uncomfortable, it may be taxing and tiring. But we make headway on holy ground when we die to ourselves and trust the Lord to be our guide.

IIIIi.IIII

So put to death the sinful, earthly things lurking within you. Have nothing to do with sexual immorality, impurity, lust, and evil desires. Don't be greedy, for a greedy person is an idolater, worshiping the things of this world. (Col. 3:5)

Run from anything that stimulates youthful lusts. Instead, pursue righteous living, faithfulness, love, and peace. Enjoy the companionship of those who call on the Lord with pure hearts. (2 Tim. 2:22)

9

Impurity from Impatience

I wish I could say that I never struggled again, sexually, following my intimacy fast. Wouldn't that make for a more clean and crisp story? I genuinely wish I could say that, after the radical ways God transformed my life, my perspective, and my heart, suddenly and immediately sexual sin was no longer a temptation for me.

Unfortunately, that wasn't the case.

After all God had done for me and all the ways He had grown me, in the face of temptation, I still chose for myself.

Can I just stop and say for a moment, "THIS IS HARD!" This life lived in obedience to God. This surrendered state of self. This Spirit-led, discerning, wisdom-guided, purity-minded, eye-ear-and-heart-guarded life is *so hard*! Please don't read a page of my story and think that for a moment I am discrediting what an immeasurable challenge this all really is. No matter how profoundly we understand the *whys* and the heart condition that compels us to obedience and purity—to walk hand in hand with a King who is holy, to be led deeper and deeper into a state of surrender by a Spirit who is almighty, to actually live in accordance to the direction and discretion of the Word of God—well, it's all just hard. I'm not denying that reality. Especially after knowing sexual immorality. After tasting what is sweet. It makes denying sexual desires all the more challenging. I've wished, so many times, I had never even given away that first kiss when I was thirteen. How much easier it would have been to not have to wrestle with turning from something I knew and, even out of the context of God's design, to a degree enjoyed. How much harder it became to be patient for His designated timing in the sexual equation when I had already experienced the carnal pleasure and rush and excitement of sexual things.

No, I'm not the picture-perfect born-again Christian. My road to sexual sanctification has been winding. I'm the story-book of messy. And still an active work in progress.

But what blew my mind then and blows my mind now—and gives me the freedom to write about my mess in this chapter of my life—is that even standing fresh in the shadow of His healing and, like a fool, again choosing sin over the Son, somehow still, like the Redeemer He is, He reached out and found me with mercy.

Here We Go Again

I was almost twenty-one months into my initially yearlong intimacy fast when I met Jeremiah. I really wasn't looking to date. But there he came—with his commanding presence and his unassuming gaze. We were introduced by a mutual friend just as soon as I moved back from LSU to Atlanta. I was content in singleness. I was focused on figuring out where God would have me as a young professional, whether He was leading me to broadcast journalism or into ministry. Whether I was supposed to plant roots in the Atlanta area or if I was best suited in another place, geographically. It was a tense and emotional season trying to navigate my way into young adulthood and allow God to sculpt in me a refined purpose and identity. The last thing I wanted to put energy toward was a man. Especially considering the sour taste I'd known from the men I'd been involved with in the past—and the sweet taste I was reveling in of a temptation-free, God-centered walk of autonomy.

But there he came. With his broad shoulders and sensitive spirit. A Goliath of a man in size who hardly knew his own appeal. His gentle nature was intoxicating. And he walked right into my singleness and sat himself down quietly.

For our first date we found our way under congested over-passes and into the drug-lorded slums of Atlanta's inner city with an outreach ministry. In just hours of knowing this man I watched him wrap his arms around the homeless and give lunches to the hungry. I learned about his childhood growing up in an Air Force family, about his time living in Zambia, Hawaii, all around the continental US, and finally settling in Colorado. I saw joy in his eyes as he told me all about his family. The second oldest of six kids. Homeschooled until he was a young teen. I watched him light up as he talked about his faith journey—his deep love for Jesus, his passion for biblical history, and his interest in discerning end-times prophecy. Then I shared about my own life as he carried conversation, effortlessly, and asked me about the things that shaped me.

At the end of the night, he hugged me.

I waved good-bye to a man who, in a single afternoon, had begun to reshape what a "man" looked like to me.

Jeremiah Lee had stepped onto my radar so effortlessly, right when I wasn't wanting or needing or looking. But after enjoying singleness for so long I was immediately conflicted by two feelings. On the one hand, I felt confident in all that God had done in my heart through my season of voluntary isolation. Pridefully, I felt like I was fully equipped and ready to step into a dating relationship. I discounted sexual sin as something I would wrestle with again. I was sure I was stronger and more capable of carrying myself with discernment and wisdom—especially considering the fact that I was now growing a ministry. In my mind I was older. Wiser. Healed and redeemed. My heart condition had shifted dramatically. We both loved Jesus and had surrendered our lives to God's leading. Surely sexual temptation wouldn't be something we needed to worry all that much about. (Who was I kidding?!)

But on the other hand I was nervous. My intimacy fast had felt so safe. My time had been my own. My energy had been my own. My full heart, mind, soul, and focus had been on Christ, alone. Sure I desired, eventually, to be a wife and a mom—which obviously required of me at some point to take a leap and date—but I really was comfortable in my unobstructed walk with the Lord. In Scripture, Paul himself talks about singleness being a blessing. A part of me wanted to cling to that and never let go. I liked being able to talk the talk and share with others the best way to live according to God's Word. But I was nervous when walking the walk would be required of me in an area I had struggled in so massively before.

I'd love to pretend I weighed the pros and cons and thought about it all for a while. But, in truth, I said yes to another date just a day or two later. And before I knew it one date had become a few and a late-night conversation by the fire on my back deck led to an innocent first kiss that broke twenty-one months of abstained physicality and, at the simplest level, triggered something in me.

Our first big error came in never truly talking about, praying about, or outlining our physical boundaries in dating. We had talked about our big-picture stance on things—the fact that neither of us believed in living together before marriage and the fact that both of us desired to abstain from sex until marriage. But prior to our first kiss we hadn't talked, in more detail, about appropriate boundaries in dating. We hadn't talked about what different triggers and temptations were for each of us and how we could best avoid them. We hadn't talked about the settings we should stay away from in order to avoid stumbling. We hadn't talked about where each of us stood on what physicality we thought was okay, or what we would do or say if we felt uncomfortable or out of control with where a situation was heading. We hadn't talked about things, in detail, that would have helped armor up our relationship to battle the inevitable temptation that would come. And since we hadn't, that first kiss led us into the battlefield blindly.

We also didn't make an intentional effort, right off the bat, to surround ourselves with supportive friends for accountability. I had arrogantly thought I wouldn't need it. But when the temptation of sexual sin became very real for me again, it was startling how much my disconnection from any accountability harmed me.

Poor Jeremiah. He really was the far more pure, innocent, and sexually unassuming one in the relationship. He had a past, but his history looked nothing like mine. In so many beautiful ways he had been taught well and led to guard his eyes, his heart, and his purity. He didn't struggle with pornography, he didn't struggle with promiscuity. He was a good man who really desired to lead well.

But me. That first kiss triggered something in me that was just overwhelming. And a sin-temptation I thought I had conquered wrapped itself up and around me again before I even knew what to think. Because I hadn't prepared myself properly and equipped myself thoroughly to stand toe-to-toe with the enemy in this specific, sensitive capacity again, I violently and voluntarily reopened so many of my grace-healed wounds. As a result, I led a good man into a rough battle he didn't deserve to have to fight.

It ultimately grew out of my own wants and my own insecurities, once again. All I had known, growing up, in my interactions with guys was how to use my sexual power to assure they were interested and would stay around. So even with a man who was wonderfully interested in me for far more than my body, it was still my ingrained response to play the sex card when I thought I needed to. So it started with teasing him. I capitalized on innocent kisses and seduced him into settings where I knew he couldn't refuse more. If he'd resist I'd manipulate the situation with my words or my teasing tone. If he'd try to lead and steer us from those things I would guilt-trip him and insist he must not really trust me or be very attracted to me. Even though he was affirming me and pursuing me so wonderfully in so many other ways, when my insecurities crawled to the surface, I still backed him into a corner time after time, physically and emotionally. And as a result, because we were both ill-equipped humans, sexual sin became routine in our story. Pressure led to permissiveness. Permissiveness led to expectancy. And expectancy eventually led to habit and routine before we even knew what had hit us.

In every other area of our relationship, things progressed beautifully. We shared so many interests, we complemented one another's personalities well, we loved one another's families. We built a solid relationship on mutual trust and great communication and the ability to be open and vulnerable, emotionally, with one another. Month after month passed and, on the surface, it seemed like we had all of the pieces in place for a long-term, enjoyable relationship. But we couldn't pretend the spiritual layer of our relationship was as idealistic and healthy as we would have liked to think. Because we were both Spirit-filled believers who actively desired to follow Jesus, the weight of the conviction we each started to feel in our sexual sin was heavy. And while before I truly surrendered my life to Christ I could have probably suppressed and rationalized that conviction until I managed to ignore it altogether, suppression of the Holy Spirit's conviction was no longer easy in my heart. After time passed and the excitement and sin-fueled rush of first pushing the boundaries faded, we were left in a place neither one of us ever wanted to be—prone to sin, embarrassed by our failings, but unsure of how to approach the whole mess of a topic without losing the other person or making the relationship more awkward and tense than it was rewarding.

That's such a hard place to be. Holding hands with a person you have grown to care for but standing at the foot of a cross that demands we give our wants up. Sexual sin is a death sentence to a freeing, Christ-centered relationship—it's a thief of genuine peace as you grow to know another's heart and they pursue your own. It complicates everything. It binds you and gags you in your attempts to lift Christ up with your life. Because, ultimately, the other person may never call you out for your part in the sexual sin that is suffocating you both, but the weight of the conviction you live with, the hypocrisy you wrestle with when your beliefs don't match your actions, and the knowledge that the love you're actually showing them is secondary to your physical wants—well, it's devastating. And it has the power to unhinge what could have been a beautiful bond with God at the center of it all.

The words of 2 Peter 2:20–22 were all too true in my own life.

And when people escape from the wickedness of the world by knowing our Lord and Savior Jesus Christ and then get tangled up and enslaved by sin again, they are worse off than before. It would be better if they had never known the way to righteousness than to know it and then reject the command they were given to live a holy life. They prove the truth of this proverb: "A dog returns to its vomit." And another says, "A washed pig returns to the mud."

The feeling was debilitating. And peace-stealing. But until we recognize that sexual acts outside of marriage are still sexual sin in the eyes of God, no matter how long we've been with our boyfriend or girlfriend, we'll continue to be living in disobedience to a God who loves us deeply and knows what's best for us. No matter how adamantly we rationalize it, justify it, or turn a blind eye to it, sexual sin—in any capacity—outside of the covenant of marriage will always hijack the full and abundant way God can operate through our lives.

Love Is . . .

So often, our impurity grows out of our impatience. At the simplest level we give pieces of ourselves away because we want to be affirmed and desire to feel seen and known and wanted. But, at a deeper level, many times we give of ourselves sexually because we genuinely long for that abiding connectedness with someone we deeply care about. Promiscuity is a layered struggle. But sexual sin in a committed relationship is a different and unique type of challenge, because it often grows out of what seems like a pure, albeit premature, place. It often grows out of a word that sexual sin steals and twists to justify our desires—*love*.

God designed sex for the very purpose of uniting two people at the most intimate and connected level—so know, first and foremost, that our desires to experience that union and intimacy are ingrained. It is what God wrote into our DNA to bind us to the spouse we take. It is beautiful, natural, and holy in so many ways.

But God also designated appropriate timing and covenantal qualifications surrounding who we would give our lives and our bodies to in that way, and in our eagerness to know that nearness to someone we care deeply for, we stumble from impatience into impurity. Then we try to justify it by stealing and confusing the definition of love—another God-defined truth we warped somewhere along the way.

We use the word *love* rather loosely these days. We love Jesus. We love that girl's hairstyle. We love our parents. We love the idea of a trip to the beach. We love our boyfriend. We love the new Netflix series we're watching. We love to play soccer. We love that paint color.

We seem to love everything. But what does love mean? Do I love Jesus the same way I love that Sherwin Williams Revere Pewter paint swatch? Probably not. (Although talk about a versatile gray!)

Do you love your boyfriend as reverently as you love God Almighty? I'm assuming no.

So what power have we lost in throwing that word around so flippantly?

What is love, *really*?

If you want to find that definition, Google Dictionary isn't the best place to look. In its attempt at wrapping words around the magnitude of love, it literally lists "have a crush on" and "idolize/worship" as synonyms, side by side. A bit broad there, don't you think? Our culture marches to the anthem of "love is love!" but leaves love without a sourced understanding. We have made *love* a relative term—open to anyone's definition. Our culture has stripped love of any absolute truth and, as a result, opened Pandora's Box in an attempt for anyone and everyone to fittingly describe it.

But, in truth, love was never ours to define. Humanity's attempt at defining love has been a long and incompetent effort to wrap insufficient words and wide-sweeping descriptions around a God-sized invention better displayed by actions than words.

Enter Jesus. Welcome the cross. It's there, in the life of Jesus and the accounts of Scripture, that we actually see love defined. In an absolute, all-inclusive, history-shifting capacity love was outlined when Jesus laid down His life for us. When the judge took on the punishment of the criminal and set the captive free.

This is real love—not that we loved God, but that he loved us and sent his Son as a sacrifice to take away our sins. . . . God is love, and all who live in love live in God, and God lives in them. And as we live in God, our love grows more perfect. So we will not be afraid on the day of judgment, but we can face him with confidence because we live like Jesus here in this world. (1 John 4:10, 16–17)

Love is patient and kind. Love is not jealous or boastful or proud or rude. It does not demand its own way. It is not irritable, and it keeps no record of being wronged. It does not rejoice about injustice but rejoices whenever the truth wins out. Love never gives up, never loses faith, is always hopeful, and endures through every circumstance. (1 Cor. 13:4–7)

God is love. God is Jesus. And Jesus is the picture of self-sacrifice for the world. So what is love if not self-sacrifice? Do we truly love another if we aren't helping to guard their heart, their body, and their spirit in purity and in obedience to God? Furthermore, do we truly love God if we aren't willing to love another by His definition and if we aren't willing to sacrifice our wants for His will?

Let love be genuine. Abhor what is evil; hold fast to what is good. Love one another with brotherly affection. Outdo one another in showing honor. (Rom. 12:9–10 ESV)

So many invested in long-term relationships profess their love for their partner, but their actions and sexual sin within their relationship contradict the very words that leave their lips. That was my story. I professed to love Jeremiah, but all the while I played a massive part in leading him into sin. I professed to love God with all of my heart—I was standing

Sex, Jesus, and the Conversations the Church Forgot

on stages speaking to crowds about laying down their lives to follow Christ, for goodness' sake—but I was a hypocrite behind closed doors, praising Him with my words but choosing my wants against His wisdom in that area of my life.

But the Word calls us to more. The Word calls us to complete surrender. If we are true followers of Christ, then until we actually repent of our sin struggles, turn from our choices, and receive forgiveness, the tension caused by that counterfeit love will crush us. And that relationship will never be able to truly honor God until we make a Scripture-demanded decision.

Option 1 or Option 2

After a while, Jeremiah and I hit a wall. We were both ensnared in the seemingly inescapable habit of our actions and equally as crushed by conviction in our actions to a degree neither of us had experienced before. I felt like Paul's words were written right to my frustrated soul:

> So the trouble is not with [God's] law, for it is spiritual and good. The trouble is with me, for I am all too human, a slave to sin. I don't really understand myself, for I want to do what is right, but I don't do it. Instead, I do what I hate. But if I know that what I am doing is wrong, this shows that I agree that the law is good. So I am not the one doing wrong; it is sin living in me that does it.
>
> And I know that nothing good lives in me, that is, in my sinful nature. I want to do what is right, but I can't. I want to do what is good, but I don't. I don't want to do what is wrong, but I do it anyway. But if I do what I don't want to do, I am not really the one doing wrong; it is sin living in me that does it.

I have discovered this principle of life—that when I want to do what is right, I inevitably do what is wrong. I love God's law with all my heart. But there is another power within me that is at war with my mind. This power makes me a slave to the sin that is still within me. Oh, what a miserable person I am! Who will free me from this life that is dominated by sin and death? Thank God! The answer is in Jesus Christ our Lord. So you see how it is: In my mind I really want to obey God's law, but because of my sinful nature I am a slave to sin. (Rom. 7:14–25)

My frustration with myself was overwhelming, but I knew the answer to all of this turmoil in me was going to be found in Jesus alone. I just had to find the courage to seek out what the Word said. When my soul collided with the Scripture that God spoke right through to my heart, it hurt. And seemed overwhelming. But if I wanted to honor God with my life, Scripture made it very clear that I had a choice to make.

In the midst of 1 Corinthians 7, which I encourage everyone to read in regard to singleness, sex, and marriage, verses 2, 8, and 9 simply and directly read, "But because there is so much sexual immorality, each man should have his own wife, and each woman should have her own husband.... So I say to those who aren't married and to widows—it's better to stay unmarried, just as I am. But if they can't control themselves, they should go ahead and marry. It's better to marry than to burn with lust."

Marry. That was option one.

Then I remembered 1 Corinthians 6:18, which declares, "Flee from sexual immorality. Every other sin a person commits is outside the body, but the sexually immoral person sins against his own body" (ESV).

Flee. That was option two.

There were no other options for me, just as there are no other options for you.

That was the hardest pill to swallow. Just as there is no power in a lukewarm walk with Christ, there is no significance in a rationalized, middle ground walk of obedience to God. I was in a sexually impure relationship and there were only two options that offered my soul freedom from the bondage it was tangled in.

Honor God by making my relationship holy in His sight, or honor God by breaking my relationship and fleeing the sin that was gripping us tight.

I fought that ultimatum for a while in my heart. Jeremiah and I talked about steps to take in order to avoid sexual sin. We set boundaries, avoided particular settings, and had deeper, tear-filled conversations about the specific catalysts that drew us in. We tried in our own might to keep our relationship God-honoring. But we just failed. Time and time again. We would make it longer and longer stretches of time without stumbling, but ultimately something would eventually trigger our lust and our sin-nature would draw us right back in. Then the cycle of shame and guilt would repeat itself until we found ourselves exhausted and at wit's end.

Matthew 10:37 is a sobering piece of Scripture because it reads, "If you love your father or mother more than you love me, you are not worthy of being mine; or if you love your son or daughter more than me, you are not worthy of being mine." We could so easily insert into that passage, "if you love your boyfriend or your girlfriend more than you love me, you are not worthy of being mine."

What Jesus is saying in that Scripture is that we are to hold no other gods before Him—not our desires, not our families, not our jobs, not our dreams, and certainly not any other relationship with any other human being. If we are in a sexual relationship and are not willing to either marry the person or to give the relationship up, then we aren't worthy of calling ourselves His followers, because we aren't actually loving God with reverent, all-consuming love. In fact, if we aren't willing to either marry the person or to give the relationship up, then by association we are willingly choosing to use the relationship to serve our own rebellious lusts and, as a result, leading the other person into sin and separation from God to fulfill our own wants.

I don't think Jesus is off in saying such strong words. Maybe we aren't worthy of being called His, in that case. Maybe we have misunderstood "love."

Jeremiah and I had a choice to make, no matter what. As intense and inconvenient and challenging as it seemed, we knew we could no longer play the back-and-forth game we'd been stuck in for so long. There was no more sin-filled middle ground in no-man's-land. No, we needed to lay it all on the table, start praying, and decide what God would have of us. Were we willing to take the crazy, faith-filled leap of a lifetime commitment to one another, or must we give up this thing we had been working and growing for so long?

IIIhIIIII

Temptation comes from our own desires, which entice us and drag us away. These desires give birth to sinful actions. And when sin is allowed to grow, it gives birth to death. (James 1:14–15)

Don't let the excitement of youth cause you to forget your Creator. Honor him in your youth before you grow old and say, "Life is not pleasant anymore." (Eccles. 12:1)

10

Unrealistic Sexpectations

I remember standing behind a grove of plants in the Costa Rican rain forest listening for my musical cue to turn the corner and stroll down the grassy aisle to my soon-to-be groom.

When faced with one of two options—flee or marry—Jeremiah and I knew that the middle ground of sin was no longer an option. We had to make a choice, no matter how hard. So we prayed separately. We prayed together. And, ultimately, we put some distance between ourselves as I headed to Joplin, Missouri, for three months to lead a missions team in some disaster relief and community aid efforts over the summer. It was during that time apart, each individually seeking God's will for our friendship, relationship, and future, that we read through Gary Chapman's *The Five Love Languages* over the phone together, experienced the longest stretch of time free of sexual sin in our entire relationship, and each had the opportunity to just breathe.

Time and time again in my story, that's when God always speaks. When I step away, allow some space, and let my white-knuckled fists loosen their grip over the control I constantly find myself desperately wanting.

I will never forget the exact moment when the Holy Spirit clearly and plainly spoke to me about Jeremiah. I was carrying a stack of flattened cardboard boxes from the basement of Watered Gardens, the shelter I was leading teams of high school students in helping to renovate. Walking through the worn-out parking lot back to the recycling dumpster where some of our homeless friends tended to camp out, God physically stopped me in my tracks. I was covered in dirt and paint, arms full of trash, among the people our society deems as the least, and it was there that God met me.

I love that He never fails to meet us in the mess—or maybe we are the ones who find Him there, when we finally choose to step away from ourselves and our wants and our desperate desire for autonomy. It's usually in the least glamorous, most humble places that we die just enough to ourselves to clear space in our muddied hearts for the presence of a holy King. It was when I willingly stepped away from the roller coaster of sexual sin and offered Him my wrecked-to-redeemed-to-wrecked-again self that it felt like He stepped in alongside me again and spoke clarity into my story.

Jeremiah is the man I have for you to marry.

It was almost audible.

The words were clear, succinct, gentle, and all-consuming. They caught me so off-guard I almost tripped over my own two feet. I hadn't been in active prayer; I hadn't been in the midst of some religious act I hoped would prove to God I was worthy enough for Him to speak to me. I was just walking, cardboard boxes in hand, with a surrendered willingness in my heart to genuinely do whatever it was He told me when He chose to reveal some clarity to me—even if it meant giving up everything. In a breath, God spoke over my life and my future—God, alone, made my decision clear for me. I couldn't believe that despite our sexual sin, despite my rebellion, despite choosing to choose for myself all over again, God was still gracious enough to offer redemption in our story. There was an unshakable peace that washed over me and, in so many ways, I immediately believed that Jeremiah would be my husband.

Whether he knew it yet or not.

If there was any doubt in my mind that it was God's impression on my heart in that parking lot versus my own thoughts and wants, it was dispelled within a week or so when I had to fly from Missouri to quickly speak at a conference in Wisconsin. I was one of three main session speakers at the event, and I found myself listening to a talk by Mark Gungor, one of the other influencers, while I was there.

The forty-five minutes I sat there and listened were stunning. It was as if God Himself were speaking through Mark's lips straight to my heart. Just in case I hadn't heard Him clearly enough in that parking lot. Just in case I didn't fully trust my own discernment in determining where that resolution originated from. Just in case I did what I always seemed to do and rationalized myself back to a middle ground to sit stagnant in confusion. He placed me in a seat in a church in the middle of Wisconsin and captivated my attention through a man I'd never met who knew nothing of my struggles or my story. And He used Mark's mouth to shape the words that perfectly elaborated on God's instruction for me in my call to faithfulness moving forward.

He spoke about marriage in a way I had never heard before. He spoke about God's intent and design for the covenant. He spoke about the partnership—the helper-and-leader teamwork that's fostered in the marital commitment. He spoke bluntly about the fallacy in following society's model—thinking some unspoken rule designates that we have to date for a certain, extended length of time before we marry. Or that it's essential to "test-drive the car before you buy it," sexually.

He spoke biblical truth that so clearly explained the cause-and-effect reasoning why we fall into sexual sin by following the timetable or "complete stability" rationalization the world models as most ideal before taking the leap of faith into a commitment. He tackled topic after topic after topic that boldly challenged the world's model, pointed straight to the Word's model, and ultimately incited the women and men throughout the audience to begin thinking for themselves and prayerfully considering who and what had shaped their thoughts around the entity and purpose of marriage, as a whole.

In summary of what was a long and layered and wisdom-filled message, he expressed this simple and blunt truth: we live in a culture that tells us we need to fully figure out our own lives first before we ever consider joining lives with another. We need to become completely financially stable and established, completely independent and self-sufficient in our labor, and completely "ready" before we ever take the leap to marry. But the problem with that model is that it works like moving from the bottom to the top of a V. The longer we go on separately establishing our own lives, our own patterns, our own foundations, our own journey, the farther apart we grow. And, as a result, the greater lengths we have to span to merge two independent lives to become beautifully dependent on one another in partnership and covenant. The longer you have lived for self, the harder it becomes to die to self. And death to self for the love of another is what biblical marriage is all about. Also, the longer we go, age-wise, in delaying the faithful step into marriage, the harder and harder it becomes physiologically, socially, and emotionally to abstain from sexual immorality. Because we are creations designed to flourish into our sexual prime at a young age, when we delay the step of marriage and chase the world's model of "independent readiness" for far too long, we deprive ourselves of the very God-honoring physical, emotional, and spiritual support our Maker intended all along.

Marriage is a massive, life-changing, covenant-making decision that carries unfathomable weight in God's eyes. Don't get me wrong; it is not something to be rushed into. And it is absolutely not something God calls every person to or chooses to bless every person with. That is holy and purpose-filled and okay too. However, it is worth personally assessing why we believe what we do about it and asking ourselves what has served to shape our understanding of the timetables, purposes, and partnership around it.

I felt like God was unhinging my soul, like somehow the pastor on the stage had some type of looking glass into my mind and knew the intimate details of my heart's cry and frustrations and confusion at the time.

I suppose that's how the Holy Spirit works, huh? It left me challenged, enlightened, and ultimately affirmed that what I had heard from God in that parking lot was not a fun idea, it was a holy breath. A divine revelation that was given to make my journey's next steps confident and courageous as I took a giant leap toward the further surrender of myself.

I didn't know if, how, or when God was going to reveal the same things to Jeremiah's heart, but He had spoken so clearly over my own life that I trusted, in His timing, He would do the same for my future groom. Because I knew God had designed me and was refining me to be Jeremiah's friend and partner and helpmate in sharing the gospel together for the rest of our lives. I crossed my fingers that God would breathe the same peace over Jeremiah's heart . . . soon!

IIIIIIIIII

Standing under that flower-strewn canopy staring into Jeremiah's eyes felt like such a surreal picture of God's faithfulness and redemption again in my life. It also felt like a step of obedience to God more than it felt like a completely emotion-led, romantic, dream-come-true moment. We were marrying because we loved one another and were the best of friends, yes. But more so than that, we were marrying because we loved God more. And we didn't want to live in burning sexual temptation and sin and disobedience any longer.

Were there butterflies? Absolutely. Were there some fluctuating doubts? At times. Did we feel completely ready in every possible, practical way in life? Not quite. But I still can't find anywhere in Scripture that talks about us having all of the answers before we respond to God's instruction in our lives. Rather I find, time and time again, the courageous call to walk by faith, not by sight. To respond in obedience and to surrender our need to have everything perfectly figured out. The truth of Scripture strips away our bargaining power with God. It says if you struggle to control yourself sexually, live in complete obedience by wedding or by fleeing. Nail sexual sin to the cross at Christ's feet. Then pick up your cross, abide, and follow Him.

So vows were shared and rings found their way around fingers, and we washed one another's feet and proclaimed that holy promise in front of friends and family. I was sure after that beautiful "I do" rolled off my lips I would finally be free of the saga of my sexual struggles. I was certain at our first moment of unity that the book was closing on my sexual testimony.

But again, who was I kidding?

When the last song finished playing at our reception and all that was left of the cake was crumbs and we found our way back to our room for the first night sleeping side by side, bride and groom, I quickly realized the book was not closing on my sexual journey. A page had simply been turned. A new chapter was beginning and I had a lot to learn.

Let me start by saying that sexual sin before marriage complicates everything. While either marriage or the complete abandonment of a relationship plagued with sexual sin are the two options Scripture draws us to, saying "I do" is not an instantaneous fix to years of sexual sin, bondage, complexity, and soul wounds. I loved Jeremiah so much and I was so overwhelmingly grateful to be his partner, his helper, and his wife. We had taken the right step in marrying, but the wedding vows weren't a cure-all for the sexual repercussions of our past that still needed to be worked through. The enemy doesn't let us off the hook that easily—no, in truth, marriage can become just as vulnerable a hunting ground for sin's relentless pursuit.

My sister-in-law shared the greatest insight with me as I was preparing to marry. She simply shared that in regard to physicality and sexuality, "Prior to marriage, the enemy does everything in his power to drive us together. And after marriage, the enemy does everything in his power to drive us apart." It wasn't but a week into our marriage that I began to see this truth rear its head and start to play out.

I think many of our sexual struggles within marriage begin with the unrealistic "sexpectations" we have for the bedroom. The enemy's first and greatest tool in dividing us is the naivety of our own minds—minds that are products of a world we've allowed to shape us. For decades of our lives we are inundated with ideas, interpretations, images, and portrayals of sex that serve to mold what we expect the act to be like in a passionate, chemistry-filled marriage. The more I've learned what others are dealing with in regard to their expectations of sex, the more I've realized that it's a wide gamut of different types of people who are all falling victim to a distorted reality shaping their lusts.

On one hand, there are those who have clung to and exalted virginity in a prideful fashion like I did in my youth. In that case, our issues begin when we are just about guaranteed by many well-meaning individuals within the church body that if we save ourselves until marriage, if we just hold out until our wedding night, until we become a bride or a groom, then the sex will be *amazing*. It is reinforced in our minds, almost as a bargaining tool, that if we are patient enough, the prize will be overwhelming. That sex will be just as God intended it and that it will be so worth it.

While this is true in many ways, it also subconsciously builds a false understanding that sex's sole purpose is to serve us. When the realities of sex and the deeper layers of the mental, emotional, and spiritual connection that make it so much more rich and connective aren't elaborated upon, it paints a false—and falsely hopeful—picture that our first time, and all subsequent sexual encounters with our spouse, will Blow. Our. Minds. We see staged and scripted versions of sex play out passionately and poetically on TV and in movies. We read about it and fantasize about the excitement and wonder of our first time. Years of daydreaming lead us to false sexpectations about how good, how pleasurable, and how completely satisfying losing our virginity will undoubtedly be.

But when we wait for the sake of waiting in hopes of a life-changing pleasure as a reward for our good works, we exalt sex as a false idol that we long to perfectly complete and fulfill us. When we are narrow-minded in our expectations of sex based solely on a tunnel-vision view of our first time being everything and more than we could ever dream up, we can fall victim to unrealistic sexpectations that will only serve to disappoint us.

(In fact, one of my motivating factors in writing this book was as a response to an article that went viral a few years back. In it, a girl blogged about how she waited until her wedding day to have sex, like she thought a "good Christian" was supposed to do, and then the sex that night, and the sex moving forward, didn't live up to her expectations. She blogged about how she, as a result, completely and totally regretted waiting. And that article was shared, liked, and reshared again for months in response. My heart just about broke in half when I saw that message spread to other frustrated, wandering, and wounded hearts. I sat back and realized how massively the church, as a whole, had failed to communicate the deeper truths of sex and the wonder of the wait. How catastrophically we failed at promoting the true *whys*. And how damaging, unmet sexpectations were able to reinforce an already raging wildfire.)

On the other hand, there are those who live through their entire season of singleness pushing the envelope constantly or giving of themselves repeatedly or seeking sexual fulfillment in every relationship they step into, never giving much thought or discretion to any sexual regulation in their life. While it would be nice to think that some advantage may come from this in the sense that people who fall into this group would be the most experienced and most seasoned, sexually, or even exempt from unrealistic sexpectations based on their practice and comfortability entangling their body and soul with others, that is not the truth. From a background of promiscuity and unrepentant, deviant sexual behavior comes other false sexpectations. Selfish sex is the by-product of this behavior, because the sexpectation is that sex is just there to serve you. Those who have never known any restraint, sexually—whether physically or by viewing pornography anytime the urge compelled them to—can step into marriage with the false sexpectation that their partner will always be able to meet their needs when they desire and just as they desire them to.

The false sexpectation that sex is designed solely to please you, to meet your needs, and to always be erotic, enticing, and adrenaline-filled can cause disappointment, tension, and complete divisiveness in marriage, especially. That kind of constant, illicit sex is just not the consistent reality when you're mingling hearts and bodies with the same person for the rest of your life, rather than unpredictable hookups or the ease of a computer screen.

A lack of sexual restraint in singleness can actually serve as one of the biggest false sexpectations in marriage. Those coming in with the most experience are surprisingly often the same ones who wrestle with the most disappointment when false sexpectations aren't met.

As for me and Jeremiah, our situation fell in a third category. Neither of us had been entirely sexually abstinent or expected our first time to complete us in some way. But neither of us had lived in unrepentant sexual sin without a second thought between partners or actions either. Rather, we fell in the middle ground, as we had operated in sexual sin in various ways but knew we were living in disobedience and wrestled deeply with conviction, guilt, and shame. So the false sexpectations that grew out of our situation were that when we married, and sex became permissible in the eyes of God and others, it would suddenly be guilt-free, easy, and liberating. I really believed that once permissibility finally escorted shame out of the equation, I would get to have my cake and eat it too. I would get an easy, fulfilling sex life without ever having to rehash the past or the guilt I had once navigated through. And while this seems idealistic and wonderful, if true, the fact is that this simplification of sex's soul-influence, as based purely on whether it's allowed or not, will leave us frustrated and confused when our actual post-sex feelings don't line up with what we hoped for or thought.

Because of the culture we live in, the density of what we are exposed to, and the conversations that have been misled or forgotten along the way, false sexpectations have become one of the enemy's greatest tools in twisting the gift of sex within marriage right from the moment we go down that aisle, hand in hand with the partner we've vowed to love all the days of our lives. And for me, at least, those false sexpectations were met with a one-two punch of reality that left me confused and, in some ways, disappointed in my early days as a bride.

Right off the bat I faced "sex guilt" nobody had prepared me for or even really mentioned leading up to my wedding. When I say sex guilt, what I really mean is the complete mental shift required of you shortly after your vows are swapped and you sneak up to the bridal suite with your new spouse. I've spoken with other friends who have wrestled with this phenomenon too. It seems to be one of the biggest conversations the church body has forgotten to share with one another, and I think it's because it requires us to be really honest on something that seems so taboo. Because of the misled conversations and the missed topics in the earliest parts of our sexual journeys, I know virgins and not-so-virgins who have all seemed to share this struggle once they've said "I do."

Whether through abstinence or a struggle with the guilt of conviction in promiscuity, for years it has been reinforced in us that sex is something you should resist, turn from, and say no to. For most of our youth and young adulthood we wrestle with desiring it but feeling ashamed of our desires. We repeatedly deny ourselves of it and, oftentimes, grow a guilt around sexuality. Because sex isn't properly introduced to us as a gift from God, an act of worship, and a holy, binding act that should be celebrated in the right context, we know sex as something scandalous and devious and guilt-carrying to desire. When a world that has inundated us with it constantly collides with a church that has only reinforced we must solely deny ourselves of it, how could we possibly just switch gears and instantly know how to celebrate it once we say "I do"?

Sex guilt was real for me. I couldn't believe that suddenly it was just "okay" to be having sex whenever and wherever my husband and I pleased. I remember thinking it was weird enough suddenly carrying the titles of husband and wife, but it was also so shocking to me that when we woke up the next morning and saw our wedding attendees as we drove back to the airport, I didn't have to be ashamed that everyone knew we had just spent the night together. The next week brought the same feelings. In the bedroom the weight of that guilt was something that kept nagging me, mentally. Even as we set off for our honeymoon I remember struggling with the guilt of being sexual and saying yes to my husband's advances, when everything conditioned in me was so used to either saying no or to feeling shameful once things were through.

That sex guilt was then followed by a repercussion of my previous sexual sin that, for years, had steadily been building a mental, physical, and spiritual barricade around my body. For years I had carelessly given myself away in every other context outside of the final physical act of sexual intercourse, yet still exalted virginity as my banner of pride and discretion. And in doing so I had always operated, sexually, in a conscious, performance-based way. Since I would never give a guy everything, I had always worked hard at sexually performing to the best of my abilities in every other way so he wouldn't be disappointed that I wasn't willing to go all the way. I gave of myself sexually, but always with an alarm in my mind that would shut me down and close off my body if things were progressing to the point I wasn't willing to go.

That warped and unhealthy means of getting what I wanted while still justifying myself served me at the time, but I never would have guessed that years later it would rear its repercussions at the most inopportune time.

As I lay in my honeymoon bed and listened to the sea right outside of our cruise ship suite, I couldn't figure out why I was so tense and why sex just wasn't blowing my mind like everyone had told me it would. My thoughts were constantly spinning. Was I pleasing him enough? Was I doing things right? How did my body look? How was I supposed to sound? Was it supposed to feel like this? Why was my body cooperative sometimes and in pain the next?

Honeymoon sex wasn't ecstasy, it was dizzying.

And to compensate for my insecurities when the sex just wasn't measuring up to all I had always been shown and thought and pictured, I activated my go-to defense mechanism to hide my insecurities and shame—and I put on a performance. I closed myself off, emotionally. I reverted to all I had previously known and I put up my "off limits" mental walls that, in turn, shut down my body physically. I tried to put on a show to convince my poor husband that it was all amazing, but I was silently ensnared by unresolved sin bondage. And I wasn't really enjoying much of anything.

False sexpectations of what sex was supposed to be, matched with a heart unprepared for how Satan was going to capitalize on my unresolved sin struggles and insecurities, completely robbed me of peace and enjoyment of sex and of my husband, ultimately. It's just simply what unrealistic sexpectations do. The virgin ends up disappointed on their wedding night because sex—especially the first time having sex—didn't measure up to the fantasy they perceived to be true. The more sexually open individual ends up disappointed and devoid of connection, subconsciously communicating to their lover that they don't measure up, because their measuring stick was impractical in the first place. They eventually get restless and become a selfish lover, depriving their partner of the wholeness of sex, because they're only ever able to operate through the lens of their own wants, their own needs, and their own view. The sexual sinner riddled with guilt is disappointed in the end when their wedding vows didn't eradicate the unresolved sin-and-shame pattern issues they never fully worked through.

Unrealistic sexpectations framed around an incomplete understanding of why and for what purpose sex was created only ever stand to leave us sexually frustrated and confused. For me, the world had screamed such a loud and drowning message at me for so many years; it wasn't until sex was actually being carried out in the appropriate, God-honoring context that the repercussions of my unrealistic views hacked away at my confidence and wasted no time in shoving us toward ruin.

I felt the constant pressure of a culture that said we should be doing it multiple times a day, every day, on our honeymoon, but I sat in the disappointing reality that neither of us could physically keep up with that. I was convinced it was my fault and invited insecurity into our sheets.

Unmet sexpectation.

I felt the constant pressure of a culture that said the pleasure should blow our minds. All the while my body was withdrawing and my spinning, suffocated mind wouldn't let me relax enough to enjoy things. I was convinced I was damaged goods.

Unmet sexpectation.

I felt the constant pressure of a culture that said sex should be erotic and intense and passionate every single time. But no matter how hard I tried to perform, that wasn't our reality, especially as we were learning each other's bodies, and because of that I was convinced our chemistry just wasn't what it should be.

Unmet sexpectation.

I had thought it would all become so easy at that altar. I had thought the sexual struggles would cease. That sex would be everything our culture had painted it to be. I had thought sex would be natural and effortless and easy—that I wouldn't ever have to rehash any of my previous struggles and deviant things.

Which category do you fall into? So few of us are exempt from false sexpectations that let us down when the reality of God's beautiful gift collides with our misinterpreted understanding of how that gift truthfully fleshes out.

Unmet sexpectations have the power to leave us reeling—and feeling like incapable, insufficient, insignificant goods.

For the first four nights of my honeymoon, I cried. Because of the enemy's stranglehold over my warped perceptions and my bondage-scarred insecurities, every evening after coming together with my new husband, whom I loved so incredibly deeply, I quietly cried myself to sleep.

IIIIiIIII

Yes, it is good to abstain from sexual relations. But because there is so much sexual immorality, each man should have his own wife, and each woman should have her own husband. The husband should fulfill his wife's sexual needs, and the wife should fulfill her husband's needs. The wife gives authority over her body to her husband, and the husband gives authority over his body to his wife.

Do not deprive each other of sexual relations, unless you both agree to refrain from sexual intimacy for a limited time so you can give yourselves more completely to prayer. Afterward, you should come together again so that Satan won't be able to tempt you because of your lack of self-control. (1 Cor. 7:1–5)

11

Sex Is Not a Sin: God's Illogical Redemption

We let our guard down so hard and so fast when we say "I do." We think it's the end of the battle of all these things we've struggled with or had to resist or fought against, sexually. But, in truth, singleness is like the on-deck circle where the batter warms up his swing before he even steps up to the plate. Marriage is the batter's box. That's where the attacks come at you before you can blink, and where the risks of getting taken out or striking out become as real as they can be. For me, spiritual temptation in singleness felt like child's play compared to the warfare inflicted in marriage. My newlywed bliss was almost outweighed by the overwhelming realization that the enemy doesn't ever rest. And that reality was taxing.

Marriage is the enemy's hunting ground—the greatest revealer of our weaknesses, our struggles, and our insecurities. It's a really good thing we love that person who stood across from us at the altar. Because the minute we get married we have one person—*one person*—whom the enemy will direct all of our frustrations, resentments, anxieties, and annoyances toward. And your spouse's toward you. Why? Because Satan gets no greater victory than seeing a husband and wife break in two. His work started when the words "I do" left your lips. In that breath he was already busy dividing you.

Marriage is the clearest picture of the gospel covenant we get the opportunity to live out. It's hard to remember that the gospel was literally Christ getting beaten, broken, and nailed to a cross. But that's what we stepped into. When we are in the throes of sexual sin in singleness there is no easy way out. I mentioned that the two options Scripture offers us are to flee or to marry. And while, on the surface, marriage seems like the easier, more emotionally fulfilling route that allows us to continue in relationship with the person we love, the reality is that in response to sin, God always requires sacrifice. It is the model of the cross. For our salvation, Jesus has paid that sacrificial price. But for our sanctification, we are called to make sacrifices too. So really the choice comes down to death to self or death to self. Death to self by denying your desires and fleeing from sin. Or death to self by laying down your life for another, sacrificially, in marriage. The voluntary willingness to live out the gospel in the covenant of marriage—the weekly, daily, hourly decision to put another before you—is glory, but it's not easy. It demonstrates a holy story, but it's not easy. It exalts the model God always intended for *love*, but it's not easy. The enemy despises the power of that promise. So we can't crave or cave to *easy*. We have to choose to take the harder road, to keep our guard up, to fight for what we know is true.

And what Jeremiah and I knew was true, as that ship swayed against the waves and our new wedding bands wrapped heavy around our fingers, was that God Himself had called us to marriage and that sex was one of God's gifts to marriage. God's gifts are good, not oppressive and burdensome. So the error in our struggles was not with sex itself, and it was not just in the false sexpectations that disappointed us. At a deeper level, we weren't receiving the magnitude of the gift God had for us in sex because we were off-base in our approach to the act that was meant to bind us. We were going at it alone, and forgetting to invite in the most crucial and overlooked element of a healthy sex life—God Himself.

Our first and most significant step toward healing began when Jeremiah stepped up in his first true act of leadership in our marriage and dragged me over to his side of the bed one honeymoon evening as I was quietly crying into our sheets. He didn't say much, he just held me. Before I knew it, he walked us into prayer together. And the heaviest moment slowly became heavenly.

Jeremiah prayed with confidence, with conviction, and with authority. He prayed words I doubt many wrap up into their bedsheets. He prayed that God would be glorified in that very moment. That my burdens would be lifted and that any chains I was feeling weighed down by would be broken in Jesus Christ's name. He prayed for me as his bride, for himself as my groom. He prayed that our sex life would be made whole and renewed. He prayed and he prayed, and my tears slowly dried as I felt a peace and a comfort flood into that tiny room. In a moment of vulnerability and desire and honesty, Jeremiah simply opened the door and invited Jesus into our bedroom.

In a humble and unassuming step, he became the first man in my entire life to realign God and sex into their rightful positions—intertwined with one another and braided together with our love story.

His gentle words felt like a declaration of Psalm 51:1–17
over our marriage that day:

> Have mercy on me, O God,
>> because of your unfailing love.
> Because of your great compassion,
>> blot out the stain of my sins.
> Wash me clean from my guilt.
>> Purify me from my sin.
> For I recognize my rebellion;
>> it haunts me day and night.
> Against you, and you alone, have I sinned;
>> I have done what is evil in your sight.
> You will be proved right in what you say,
>> and your judgment against me is just.
> For I was born a sinner—
>> yes, from the moment my mother conceived me.
> But you desire honesty from the womb,
>> teaching me wisdom even there.
> Purify me from my sins, and I will be clean;
>> wash me, and I will be whiter than snow.
> Oh, give me back my joy again;
>> you have broken me—
>> now let me rejoice.
> Don't keep looking at my sins.
>> Remove the stain of my guilt.
> Create in me a clean heart, O God.
>> Renew a loyal spirit within me.
> Do not banish me from your presence,
>> and don't take your Holy Spirit from me.
> Restore to me the joy of your salvation,
>> and make me willing to obey you.
> Then I will teach your ways to rebels,
>> and they will return to you.

> Forgive me for shedding blood, O God who saves;
>   then I will joyfully sing of your forgiveness.
> Unseal my lips, O Lord,
>   that my mouth may praise you.
> You do not desire a sacrifice, or I would offer one.
>   You do not want a burnt offering.
> The sacrifice you desire is a broken spirit.
> You will not reject a broken and repentant heart,
>   O God.

In that moment I felt more unified with my husband than I ever had before. And it felt like his humble words had somehow accessed the power to unshackle the Holy Spirit from the self-inflicted bondage I had suppressed it with, again, in that season of life. The power and freedom of God coursed through my heart that day, just by the words of a genuine prayer from the hurting heart of a new groom. Jesus entered into our marital sex life and began to restore already fractured pieces and make things new.

In the days following Jeremiah's open invitation for Christ to enter our sex life, God began to remind me of and clarify truths to my heart that I had been mindless of. The first was simple but could not be overstated enough to my poorly conditioned, worn-out heart: sex was not a sin. In the right context, it was the ultimate act of worship. A beautiful expression of unity between a husband and a wife and a holy act meant to bring two people together in vulnerability, surrender, and dependence. Sex was worth celebrating in marriage! Worth exploring and uncovering and delighting in.

This is another conversation the church has forgotten to delight in. We talk a lot about abstinence. A lot about avoidance. A lot about the repercussions of sexual sin. But we completely miss the mark in exalting the gift of sex! We miss the mark in sharing how awesome, exciting, pleasurable, and unifying sex is in marriage. When sex is carried out as God designed it to be delighted in, it is hard to find the words to wrap around the deep and unhinging glory that unity brings. The church seems too often to direct all of its sexual preaching toward the singles and forgets to pour into the wedded couples the truth that sex is not a sin. Your husband is a gift to you from God. Your wife is a gift you are free to delight in. Sex is worship, and wonderful, even through the growing pains and the trial-and-error learning curve that come early on in marriage.

Someone once told me, in layman's terms, that in response to an enemy whose sole goal is to drive a husband and wife apart, sex is actually the ultimate middle finger to sin. A pleasurable, formidable, and confident act that reminds Satan of his place. An act that God actually commands us to in marriage, because he knows the power sex has in our bodies, minds, and hearts to unify us and strengthen us for the days that lie ahead. Sex is a reminder to the enemy that you are not soon divided. That he doesn't get to win.

Shortly after marrying, Jeremiah and I read about a couple whose young child unexpectedly died. In their testimony they shared that the first thing they did on the night they found out about their baby's life abruptly ending was come together and have sex. They did this, in the darkest and hardest moment of their lives, to remind themselves and to remind the enemy that they were unified, even in grief. Because God's gifts are perfect. And holy. And never so simple or vanilla as to only serve one purpose or be used for one thing. Sex is a tool for worship—a weapon against Satan's schemes.

As the church, we've forgotten to talk about *that* sex. We've forgotten to celebrate and edify and exalt that gift God designed to weld us together in spirit and decimate the enemy's chance at any victory. That sex, that holy, covenant-bound sex is what's worth waiting for. That sex is what God always intended it to be—shame-free, pleasure-drenched, and deeply unifying. That sex unmasks the one-night stands and the culture-crazed hookups and the promiscuity carried out in the darkness for what they really are—primitive, self-serving, impatient splurges that cheapen the value of the gift we've been given.

Genesis 2:23–25 finds Adam, the very first man, in awe of the partner God created him in Eve.

"At last!" the man exclaimed.

> "This one is bone from my bone,
>   and flesh from my flesh!
> She will be called 'woman,'
>   because she was taken from 'man.'"

This explains why a man leaves his father and mother and is joined to his wife, and the two are united into one. Now the man and his wife were both naked, but they felt no shame.

And Matthew 19:6 goes on to reiterate, "Since they are no longer two but one, let no one split apart what God has joined together."

Sex is not a sin within the context of marriage; it is the very act that unifies us as one flesh. One team. One force in this life. There is no shame to be had. There is no guilt that has the authority to own any piece of your redeemed and covenant-covered sexual story. Sex is God's. And God has gifted it to us.

Sex is not sin—so the only thing framing that misconception is unrepentant sin in us that we're allowing to win.

It also became clearer and clearer to me that the entire process of God's call to purity in singleness is not just to preserve a righteous and clean reputation. It is to equip us before the trials by fire come. To prepare us while we're on deck so we know how to read the pitcher and time our swings when it's our turn to step up to the plate. God calls us to surrender and to self-control in singleness because surrender and self-control in marriage are required of us every single day. Sex is not a performance-based or self-serving act that is purely there to serve our own individual wants. It is the ultimate act of service to our partner. It's an act of genuine love and generosity and vulnerability with the one we love. Ephesians 5:21 even calls us, as husband and wife, to submit to one another out of reverence for Christ.

If we don't choose to submit our lives to God in singleness or dating relationships, we won't know how to submit to one another in unity and marriage. Singleness is our training ground in discipline and perseverance. Struggles with sexual deviance in singleness only reflect a lack of self-control that will inevitably rear itself in marriage when the true tests from the enemy come.

No, sex is powerful. And purposeful. And pure in its design.

The more Jeremiah and I invited Christ into our bedroom, believed God had the power to break the chains and forgive us of the bondage-forming actions in our single lives, and delighted in sex as an act of worship as husband and wife, the more our sex life improved and thrived. There was beauty in coming together spiritually, first, because it opened the door for us to come together physically and emotionally as we found our sexual rhythm and learned to openly communicate moving forward.

We found freedom in remembering that sex wasn't, isn't, and should never be taboo between a husband and a wife. It's not shameful—it's nothing God turns His eyes from. It is something He delights in in the right context. It trumps conviction with holy connection. We even enjoy playing worship music in the background, sometimes, when we join together as husband and wife. I personally think everyone should see how things change in their intimacy when the invitation is extended to Christ to enter *every* area of their marriages and their lives—including the bedroom.

Unfulfilled sexpectations paralyzed me for a while. But the Holy Spirit broke through my misconceptions to remind me that the reality of sex is a beautiful, evolving, sacrificial act that is about so much more than our own pleasures. It's the gospel lived out in sacrificial love for another's body, soul, and heart. Sometimes it's passionate and romantic, sometimes we laugh the whole way through. Sometimes it's spontaneous, sometimes it's planned, sometimes it's completely undesired but you lay down your body anyway because you know your partner needs you. Sometimes it's lightning fast, and sometimes you waste the whole day delighting in your groom. Sometimes it's to music and sometimes it's to the background noise of your kid squealing in another room. And it's definitely a lot of different things than the sex you see on TV and in the movies. But that's the best part. Because sex in marriage is perfectly and beautifully reserved for just the two of you.

Sometimes it's remembering that every single time you let down your walls, pull back your defenses, and come together with your partner in the bedroom, it's the metaphorical middle finger at the enemy's schemes and lies that feels the most pleasurable and fulfilling to you.

IIIIiIIII

I don't understand God.

I'm not sure that I want to.

I think it's awe-inspiring that the wonder of His love for us makes no sense.

It leaves me spellbound that the same God who used Rahab in the lineage of Jesus Christ still involves Himself completely in our sexual stories.

Rahab was the prostitute. She was the damaged goods. She was the strung out and run through body-merchant that the world turned its nose up at. She was the harlot whose reputation preceded her. And still God chose to use her for the work He desired to do. Still God looked past the symptoms of her misguided heart and used her character, her faithfulness, and her humble fear of the Lord to shift the course of history. Then, to take it a step further, because God is simply the wonder-worker of illogical glory, He used a woman like Rahab in the genealogy of Jesus. The Savior of the world born from the family line of a once-desperate, broken girl.

A whore justified by faith. I suppose in a way I can relate. And for that I am all the more grateful to the King who is ready and willing to redeem our stories.

We are such a work in progress, Jeremiah and I. We don't have it all figured out in our sexual journey as husband and wife. As I write this, we are only three years into marriage, not that much further removed from the promiscuity of my youth. And closer still to our own sexual struggles that tangled us up in dating and the early days after "I do." But when I look at myself in the mirror these days, I'm constantly reminded of Psalm 103:12. God is not a keeper of our record of wrongs. He is not counting the days since our struggles subsided as a time-based gauge for how much "better" we've become. No, I'm reminded of how that Scripture clarifies, "He has removed our sins as far from us as the east is from the west." That "the LORD hears His people when they call to Him for help. He rescues them from all their troubles" (34:17). That, as Daniel 10:12 reminds us, since the first day we began to pray for understanding and to humble ourselves before our God, our requests were heard in heaven.

So the cry of my heart was, and continues to remain, "For the honor of your name, O LORD, forgive my many, many sins" (Ps. 25:11). "Do not remember the rebellious sins of my youth. Remember me in the light of your unfailing love, for you are merciful, O LORD" (v. 7).

It continues to blow me away that He has, does, and will continue to respond to our humble cries. When fear creeps in and reminds me of who I used to be, the things I have seen and tried and done, and the fact that a number of people out there could try to hold over me what they know about my past, my behaviors, and my reputation, I lean into the power of the Word and the strength of what it reminds me.

Against the fear of what others could say or what others might think or what shame might try to recapture me with, Micah 7:8–10 frames my anthem of victory.

Don't gloat over me, my enemies! For though I fell, I rose again. Though I sat in darkness, the Lord was my light. I will be patient as the Lord punishes me, for I sinned against Him and against my own body. But when the repercussions of my sins subside, He is always faithful to take up my case and give me justice and freedom. The Lord brought me into the light, and I have seen His righteousness. No matter what others try to forge against me, or what the enemy tries to leverage against me, I will not be afraid. They will see that the Lord is on my side.

Romans 8:1 declares, "So now there is no condemnation for those who belong to Christ Jesus." I wonder if that could become the new truth we allow to be etched across our healing hearts? Always remembering—even in our weaknesses, our struggles, and the painful process of dying to self and turning from sin-filled sexual things—"Once again you will have compassion on us. You will trample our sins under your feet and throw them into the depths of the ocean!" (Mic. 7:19).

I don't blame the conversations that the church forgot as the catalysts of the roller-coaster ride that was my sexual testimony. I don't blame the men involved. I don't blame the pain others caused. I don't blame the father who abandoned me. I don't blame TV or movies or music or social media. I don't blame friends. I don't blame family. I don't even blame a world that force-fed me dark and broken things.

My sexual struggles were a result, from the very beginning, of my sin-nature. My wants. My thoughts. My actions. My pride. My choices. My rebellion. My desperation for affirmation. My desires. My decision to make myself the god of my own story.

The conductor of my decades-long sexual train wreck was *me.*

But I, my friend, have been redeemed.

And again, I say, redeemed indeed.

Conclusion

The content in these pages bears just about all of myself I have to give—and handing over some of these words was a hard fight.

I dreamed of writing this book for years. But as I began to put words on the page it felt like the reality of writing it all was so much safer as a dream. That's the tricky part of handing over our lives for His exaltation, isn't it? We long for the adventure, but sometimes the adventure feels overwhelming when He calls us to step into it. Sometimes obedience is hard when it's our own weaknesses we're asked to boast in for His glory.

The hard but holy news? We are never promised safety in our journey. We are never promised total ease. We are promised love and life and freedom in His grace and strength and truth. We are promised His hedge of protection. His comfort in our vulnerability. His use of our messy things.

I'm grateful for the God-sized courage He breathes into our stories. And that His will shall be done no matter our apprehension or discomfort in the momentary process. I truly do believe God has unbelievable plans for this book.

It's my prayer that somewhere through these pages God plants seeds in your heart, whispers His loving truth to your spirit, or reaches out and, as only He can, captivates you. I hope He uses my messy words to connect with hurting hearts and peel back layers of pain and draw even the most scabbed of hearts to repentance and healing through His immeasurable grace. I hope, through these pages, He does that for you. And I hope this book inspires courage in you too.

We all have a story. We all have testimonies. Even the most seasoned of believers are still weathering life's storms. But we are all invited to share these in the confidence that He will use our open hands and hearts to draw others to their knees. Even when it's hard. Even when it's scary. In fact, when we find the courage to surrender our sexual struggles to God and allow Him to transform our mess into a message and our tests into a testimony, we gain victory over an enemy who would love nothing more than for us to stay drowned in our shame and guilt and sexual confusion.

I sense victory. In your life and in the life of anyone who makes it to these back pages. Because you've already proven you had the courage and perseverance to make it through the hard and uncomfortable words we would all rather resist and turn from. Now the kingdom needs *your* words too. I hope you'll hand your life and your sexual journey to God—because there are lives out there waiting to hear of His redemption through *you*.

I'm not sure it will ever cease to blow my mind how passionately, patiently, and mercifully God pursues us. To be honest, it doesn't make sense. Time after time His mercy still meets us. And somehow, even in our sin, it finds us again.

I pray you know redemption is waiting for you too. You are not too far gone. You are not too messy, too broken, too impure, too unclean. You are seen, known, loved, and pur-posed for a life free of the bondage of sexual sin. The leap of faith is wild. It's countercultural, laughed at, and resolve-testing. But the grace you jump into is liberating, satisfying, and soul-resuscitating.

You are braver than you know. Even in the tangles of the bondage you know. If you take away anything from this book, from these chapters, from my messy baggage-carrying words, please let it be this: you are loved. Fashioned beautifully. Cre-ated with purpose. Value-carrying. You are an image-bearer of God Almighty. A temple for His Holy Spirit. You are important. You are strong. And your crimson stains are waiting to be washed white as snow.

You are not defined by your past. You are not defined by your number. You are not defined by the sexual sin you've lived in or the sexual sin others have dragged you into. You are not imprisoned by a reputation. You are not stamped with the titles the world says you must carry. You do not have to be bound by the chains of sin struggles, soul ties, bad relation-ships, or unhealthy patterns. You are seen and cherished, and forgiveness is extended to you.

Humble yourself before the Lord.

You rebel heart, come home.

Finally, dear brothers and sisters, we urge you in the name of the Lord Jesus to live in a way that pleases God, as we have taught you. You live this way already, and we encourage you to do so even more. For you remember what we taught you by the authority of the Lord Jesus.

God's will is for you to be holy, so stay away from all sexual sin. Then each of you will control his own body and live in holiness and honor—not in lustful passion like the pagans who do not know God and his ways. (1 Thess. 4:1–5)

To conclude these pages with my own words would cheapen the wonder of a journey full of hard lessons learned. So I'll let Paul's words speak for me. I hope you know these words are patiently waiting to be the anthem of your story too.

I thank Christ Jesus our Lord, who has given me strength to do his work. He considered me trustworthy and appointed me to serve him, even though I used to blaspheme the name of Christ. In my insolence, I persecuted his people. But God had mercy on me because I did it in ignorance and unbelief. Oh, how generous and gracious our Lord was! He filled me with the faith and love that come from Christ Jesus.

This is a trustworthy saying, and everyone should accept it: "Christ Jesus came into the world to save sinners"—and I am the worst of them all. But God had mercy on me so that Christ Jesus could use me as a prime example of his great patience with even the worst sinners. Then others will realize that they, too, can believe in him and receive eternal life. All honor and glory to God forever and ever! He is the eternal King, the unseen one who never dies; he alone is God. Amen. (1 Tim. 1:12–17)

Acknowledgments

To my King—holy, holy, holy. You are good and You are holy. Jesus, You are worthy to be praised. Hallowed be Your precious and holy name. You are the greatest Author, the One who writes the most beautiful stories. God, thank You for loving us. For sending Your Son to die for us. For raising Him in victory. For seeing us. For knowing us. For calling us. And for redeeming us. Even in my filth You found me. You invited this blind, wandering heart to a place of surrender, and I am forever grateful. I am grateful for Your grace and for Your mercy. For Your empowerment through the Holy Spirit. For Your constant invitation into the wild and wonderful ways You do things. In response to what I fail to grasp I trust that You will use me. In my adversity You sustain me; You maintain me and proclaim me capable of carrying this beautiful gift of life. Thank You for trusting me with the responsibility of sharing Your truth. Thank You for the opportunity to write about the power of a life sacrificed to obedience in Your authority. May I always cling to the truth of Your holy and unfailing Word. May my opinion never trump Your instruction. May Your name ever be on my lips, Jesus. And may I choose every day to die to myself for Your glory. I am Yours.

To Jeremiah—my best friend. I couldn't have dreamed you up. You are God's clearest picture of the better, best, and immeasurably more He has for us when we pursue Him with all of our hearts and surrender our lives to His will and leading. You are more than I even knew to pray for. If I could take back every kiss I'd ever given I would. I should have saved them all for you. I'm grateful for you. For the sacrifices you make for me. For the sacrifice you make of me when you know I'm needed elsewhere too. You didn't ask for this. For a wife whose mission field is ever-changing and always seems a flight away. For the nights we fall asleep in separate beds across the country and miss the way our limbs tangle together and our love seems to breathe between the sheets. Thank you. For letting me stretch out my wild and wandering wings. For letting God use me as He needs. For pouring out alabaster grace on my travel-weary feet. We're new at this, you and me. But the way you slide your arm beneath my pillow and hold my hand as we drift off—it reminds me we'll be at this for a while. Because when I wake in the middle of the night and my fingers ache and I realize our hands are still intertwined tight, I stare at the man who first chose me. And I choose, in return, to never let go of the covenant that's holding us tight. You've made a woman out of me. And *I love you, deeply.*

Thank you for loving me despite my past—for trusting in the God who reaches into the pit to pull us from the mire and rebuild us in His image. I am a wild work in progress, and even still you champion me on. Your love coaxes the best from me. Thank you so much for working so hard for our family. Thank you for leading us with such humility and simplicity.

For allowing me to boast in my weaknesses so that others might see the glory of renewal at the cross—even when those weaknesses expose pieces of your life too. You are trusting, faith-filled, bold, sacrificial, and courageous. Where you go, I will follow, my groom. I love you.

To my Audie Lou Lou Lemonsteen Lemondrop Verbena— you are my delight, sweet baby girl. Thank you for making me a mommy. Thank you for enhancing our lives in such an immeasurable way. Thank you for letting mama sneak away for a few hours each day to write. And for always welcoming me back with kisses and snuggles and squeals. You make life that much brighter. I pray you know, from the earliest age, your worth, value, beauty, and measure in God's eyes. I pray you know you were died for. And that your purity was of utmost importance when Christ took that cross. You were created for such a time as this. It is my greatest honor to see how God uses your life each and every day. I love you, deeply.

(And to the new little bundle of joy who took up womb-and-board in my belly as I was writing this book—I'm so glad you have been growing in life as this book has come to life too. We love you so much and can't wait to meet you!)

To Amy Beth—oh my goodness, you are heaven-sent. I genuinely could not have pulled this off without you. Thank you so much for packing up your bags and taking the most massive leap of faith from Colorado to Atlanta to serve our family while I wrote this book. Your help with Auden, your investment in our crazy little clan, your service with my ministry—it has all been so invaluable to our lives. Your excitement about what I was writing helped fuel my creativity and enthusiasm when the words were hard to find and the content was heavy to pen. Your purity of heart, your genuine pursuit of righteous living, and your integrity as a woman in this wild world are not only God-honoring and Jesus-glorifying but unbelievably inspiring to me. I look up to you so much, Amy. Your life and your holy patience remind me that there is hope—hope that women will hear the truth and love of God's direction and not have to test the waters to learn from experience and pain. You are an absolute treasure—more precious than rubies. Always know that.

To Bill, Teresa, and Rebekah—my team! I could not ask for a better inner circle cheering me on, believing in my crazy writing dreams, and helping me navigate how to best paint the wild words in my heart onto each page. Thank you for team trips to the Oregon coast, for letting me into the vulnerable places in your hearts and stories, and for always understanding my priority of a family-first life. Here's to homemade crepes, rocky jetties, and another bestseller!

To Louie, Shelley, and the Passion family—your leadership and, more importantly, your friendship, have meant so much to our family. Thank you for stewarding your calling so faithfully, for always offering encouragement and championing our dreams, and for pointing all back to Jesus time and time again. We are honored to share in this life with you all and grow under your Spirit-led, Jesus-centered, King-exalting guidance.

Last but not least, to each woman persevering in purity, faithfulness, discipline, and redemption—you are really doing it! You are known, loved, and a light in this shadowed world. You are an example-setter and a leader to women all around the globe struggling with the weight of the world's twisted messages on their shoulders. You are carrying a beautiful commissioning—so walk strong. When you see a friend wandering, I hope you'll be brave enough to share with them the hope and satisfaction you know in Christ. You are a leader. You are the woman I wish I could have always been. I admire you, respect you, love you, and am so fiercely proud of you. In a world flooded with temptation, warped truth, and mixed messages, you keep your gaze set. Keep your eyes set on a King who calls you to more. A King who fulfills every desire of your heart and every need of your flesh. You are a fierce and grace-filled warrior. Fight on in faith, sister. You are seen.

Notes

Chapter 1 Let's Call It Like It Is

1. Tim Challies, "10 Ugly Numbers Describing Pornography Use in 2017," *Challies*, April 11, 2017, https://www.challies.com/articles/10-ugly-and-up dated-numbers-about-pornography-use/.

2. "Abstinence Statistics," *Statistic Brain*, accessed August 9, 2017, http://www.statisticbrain.com/abstinence-statistics/.

3. "Online Dating Statistics," *Statistic Brain*, accessed August 9, 2017, http://www.statisticbrain.com/online-dating-statistics/.

4. "Sexting Statistics," *Statistic Brain*, accessed August 9, 2017, http://www.statisticbrain.com/sexting-statistics/.

5. "Premarital Pregnancy Statistics," *Statistic Brain*, accessed August 9, 2017, http://www.statisticbrain.com/premarital-pregnancy-statistics/.

Chapter 4 You Are What You See

1. "What You See Is What You Do: Risky Behaviors Linked to Risk-Glorifying Media Exposure," *American Psychological Association*, March 7, 2011, http://www.apa.org/news/press/releases/2011/03/risky-behavior.aspx.

2. Peg Streep, "What Porn Does to Intimacy: 3 Studies Find That Explicit Material Can Do More Harm Than Most People Think," *Psychology Today*, July 16, 2014, https://www.psychologytoday.com/blog/tech-support/2014 07/what-porn-does-intimacy.

3. "Pornography Statistics: 2015 Report," *Covenant Eyes*, accessed August 9, 2017, http://www.covenanteyes.com/pornstats/.

4. Ibid.

5. Carolyn C. Ross, "Overexposed and Under-Prepared: The Effects of Early Exposure to Sexual Content: Is the Internet Impacting Sexual

Development?" *Psychology Today*, August 13, 2012, https://www.psychol ogytoday.com/blog/real-healing/201208/overexposed-and-under-prepar ed-the-effects-early-exposure-sexual-content.

6. "Dopamine," *The Dopamine Project*, accessed August 9, 2017, http:// dopamineproject.org/dopamine/.

About the Author

Well, if you made it this far in the book then you probably already know a lot more about the author than you bargained for. Ha! Thank you so much for reading. If you want to dig into more about how God interrupted my life and revealed to me the radical, heart-changing love of Jesus, you can grab a copy of my *New York Times* bestselling book, *Wreck My Life: Journeying from Broken to Bold*.

I should probably tell you a few things about me now that don't actually have to do with sex. My greatest blessing on this side of heaven is the smokin' hot man who chose me to be his bride. Jeremiah Lee Aiken is so far out of my league it's criminal, and I wake up every morning honored to be his helper, his teammate, his wife, and the mother of his children (Okay, that kind of had to do with sex . . .). But speaking of those babies, we live in Atlanta, Georgia, with our spunky daughter, Auden Noelle, and have another nugget on the way! Motherhood is the most wild, wonderful, and miraculous adventure. The primary miracle being that we've somehow managed to successfully keep tiny humans alive and thriving. (Shout out to the stay-at-home and work-from-home moms out there. You are seen, known, and admired. Families are built upon the unseen, selfless sacrifices of mothers and wives and We. Are. Rockstars!)

I am also a professional speaker and have the amazing privilege of traveling around the country and the world sharing the gospel and speaking into topics near to my heart. I'm the world's most inconsistent blogger at moisom.com, I post excessive pictures of my offspring on Instagram, and I regularly crave s'mores, watermelon, and baked sweet potatoes. (Then again, I'm regularly pregnant these days so that might have something to do with it.)

In my former life I was an All-American, record-setting goalkeeper for the LSU women's soccer team and the first female to ever train with and try out for an SEC men's football team. I was also the first female athlete to ever be crowned LSU's homecoming queen. I've appeared on *Ellen*, ESPN, CBS, Fox, *The 700 Club*, and countless other television, radio, and digital platforms. But one of the coolest things, to me at least, is that I also once climbed to the summit of Mt. Kilimanjaro. I love to be outdoors, explore the world with my family, and create elaborate voices, personalities, and backstories for my pets. (I know I'm not the only one who does that; don't even try to roll your eyes.)

We attend and serve at Passion City Church and are beyond grateful for the incredible leadership and community within our church family. To grow in a house that exalts Jesus above all, clings to the truth of Scripture, and extends itself and its resources around the city, nation, and world is truly an honor.

Enough about me; I would love to hear from you and about you! How did this book challenge or encourage you? What areas of your life did these words speak into? Please don't be shy to reach out. You can connect with me through any of the outlets below. Also feel free to jump over to my blog to read more of my writing, watch some of my videos, and discover if I'm speaking near you anytime soon. I would love to meet you and wrap a hug around your neck. Can't wait to connect!

Twitter: www.twitter.com/Molsom
Instagram: www.instagram.com/Molsom
Facebook: www.facebook.com/TheMolsom
Website: www.Molsom.com

. CONNECT WITH .

Mo Isom

🐦 @MoIsom

📘 TheMoIsom

📷 @MoIsom

▶️ Momonstr

If you're interested in booking Mo to speak at your next event or would like to check her availability and fee schedule,

VISIT MOISOM.COM

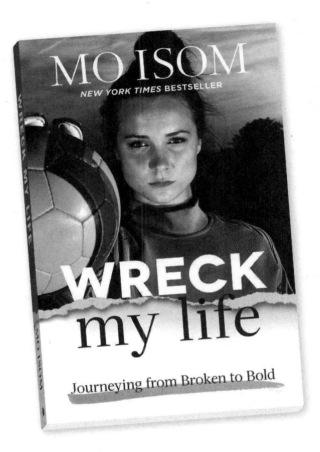

LIKE THIS
BOOK?
Consider sharing it with others!

- Share or mention the book on your social media platforms. Use the hashtag **#SexAndJesus**.

- Write a book review on your blog or on a retailer site.

- Pick up a copy for friends, family, or anyone who you think would enjoy and be challenged by its message.

- Share this message on **INSTAGRAM** and **TWITTER**: "I loved #SexAndJesus by @MoIsom"

- Share this message on **FACEBOOK**: "I loved #SexAndJesus by @TheMoIsom"

- Recommend this book for your book club, workplace, class, or church.

- Follow Baker Books on social media and tell us what you like.

 Facebook.com/ReadBakerBooks

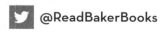 @ReadBakerBooks